Lincolnshire
COUNTY COUNCIL

discover libraries

This book should be returned on or before the due date.

NEI
05116

2 4 MAY 2019

14 AUG

13 SEP

11 OCT

8 NOV

WITHDRAWN FOR SALE LINCOLNSHIRE COUNTY COUNCIL

To renew or order library books please telephone 01522 782010
or visit https://lincolnshire.spydus.co.uk
You will require a Personal Identification Number.
Ask any member of staff for this.

The above does not apply to Reader's Group Collection Stock.

D0177073

CARS
WE LOVED IN THE
1980s

Giles Chapman

The
History
Press

First published 2014
Reprinted 2015

The History Press
The Mill, Brimscombe Port
Stroud, Gloucestershire, GL5 2QG
www.thehistorypress.co.uk

© Giles Chapman, 2014

The right of Giles Chapman to be identified as
the Author of this work has been asserted in
accordance with the Copyrights, Designs and Patents Act 1988

All rights reserved. No part of this book may be reprinted
or reproduced or utilised in any form or by any electronic,
mechanical or other means, now known or hereafter invented,
including photocopying and recording, or in any information storage
or retrieval system, without the permission in writing from the Publishers.

British Library Cataloguing in Publication Data.
A catalogue record for this book is available from the British Library.

ISBN 978 0 7509 5845 5

Typesetting and origination by The History Press
Printed in China.

Introduction

You may not have even noticed it, but many of the cars in this book are no longer around in large numbers. See a Citroën Visa, an Audi 100, a Fiat Uno or a Nissan Bluebird in a supermarket car park and it'll stop you in your tracks.

The 1980s was certainly the era when interest in classic cars soared. But while we were busy celebrating old favourites from the 1950s and '60s, we never bothered to think that popular modern models would, some day, be just as fascinating. So once our '80s cars – with their plastics and early digital displays and electric gadgets – had passed through several households, lost a few functions and, finally, flunked their MoT tests, it was off to the scrapyard and an eventual smelting. No doubt the same careless fate will befall cars from subsequent decades.

Yet no matter what your personal experience of the '80s, it was an extremely important and vibrant time for the car industry. If you were a high performance freak, then it was the era of turbochargers, multi-valve engines and hot hatchbacks, and the insane idea that a production car could exceed 200mph. Then again, if you were more concerned with fuel efficiency then it was a time when diesel cars gained huge significance. The rapid spread of four-wheel drive and anti-lock brakes were to the safety benefit of all drivers, while the gradual introduction of airbags made cars much less dangerous for occupants.

The car market settled into a soon-familiar pattern of sectors that every major player had to adhere to: compact superminis like the Peugeot 205, family hatchbacks exemplified by the Ford Escort MkIII, mid-range saloons such as Vauxhall's Cavalier, executive cars where the BMW 5 Series excelled, and luxury saloons typified by the Mercedes-Benz S Class and Jaguar XJ6. Sports cars went mid-engined and many apparently different cars started to share identical hidden 'platforms'.

But there were intriguing new classes of car generating huge interest: first the people-carrier and later the four-wheel drive sport-utility vehicle.

You'll find all these cars, and many others, in this unique celebration of 1980s motoring. You'll also relive the introduction of unleaded petrol, the opening of the M25, the ongoing battle to dominate the sales chart, the way the Audi Quattro redefined the supercar, and how the route was paved for the British driver in the 1990s. Mostly, though, this book highlights the attainable cars we loved in the rollercoaster '80s, and will re-acquaint you with many of the models that, perhaps, you'd forgotten about – and probably won't have even seen for a good few years. We begin in the very late 1970s, when several '80s classics were just emerging. Turn the page to fire up the first one.

Citroën Visa, 1978

Citroën's *entrée* into the supermini class was a welcome extension of choice for anyone needing a compact, cheap-to-run little car. This was an unusual contender because only a five-door layout was offered – very useful with that hatchback opening right down to bumper level. Revealed in autumn 1978, Visas arrived at Britain's Citroën dealers in spring 1979.

Something else setting the car apart from the herd was its choice of two- or four-cylinder engines. The raucous, air-cooled flat-twin had a slightly bigger capacity, 652cc, than in the Dyane and 2CV and, although it could muster only 35bhp, it meant a Visa could be maintained on a shoestring.

The four-cylinder engine, meanwhile, was a water-cooled 1.1- or

WHAT THEY SAID AT THE TIME

'The Visa is an amalgam of Citroën and Peugeot components, but the result is pure Citroën. Its flat-twin 650cc engine endows it with only a moderate performance, but ride, accommodation and refinement are virtues.'

Motor magazine in October 1979 on the £2,950 Visa Club.

1.2-litre unit, and it betrayed the Visa's roots because it was shared with the Peugeot 104. In fact, the whole car was based around a 104 floorpan and running gear to save costs. This certainly watered down Citroën's usual idiosyncratic character – the Visa had conventional springs in its suspension, rather than a complex hydropneumatic system. It was the beginning of the end, really, for the marque's independent engineering flair.

Externally, though, the Visa was unmistakeably Citroën, with its aerodynamic frontage, semi-concealed rear wheels and single-spoke steering wheel and drum controls rather than stalks on the column. In the early 1980s came a gutsy 1.7-litre diesel engine, a novel convertible with a peel-back roof, and a boxy van edition, the C15, which was on sale until 2005 … out-living its passenger-carrying sisters by an incredible seventeen years!

Couldn't be anything other than a Citroen, even though it was based on the Peugeot 104. This is a 1979 Visa Super.

Idiosyncratic controls featured a single-spoke steering wheel and fingertip-operated functions on drums rather than stalks.

WHO LOVED IT?

Budget-conscious French motorists wanted something more modern than the Citroën 2CV and Renault 4, and they found it here. A stratum of British car buyers liked the highly practical Visa, too, although the zany interior was off-putting to many.

Renault 18, 1978

Conventional, large family cars remained the most popular choices among Britain's drivers, and the Cortina, Cavalier and their ilk had a deadly serious new rival in the smooth shape of this new Renault, first on British sale in spring 1979.

Instead of French quirks, it offered all-round competence. The interior was spacious and stylish, there was a new 1.4-litre engine with a plucky 64bhp for the starter versions, and pliant MacPherson strut front suspension. The TS and GTS came with a 1.6-litre engine and four- or five-speed gearboxes respectively.

In very short order, a diesel engine option, an estate derivative, and a 2.0-litre executive model were added, but the most interesting spin-off was the Turbo, on sale in 1981. Renault pioneered turbocharging in Formula 1 racing in 1977 and now the 18 Turbo was turned into its first turbocharged production car. The Garrett T3 turbo was attached to a 1.6-litre engine to put 125bhp of power at the driver's disposal. There was a five-speed gearbox, power steering, wacky-looking alloy wheels and a tail spoiler. It was a 120mph car but, with all that urge going

WHAT THEY SAID AT THE TIME

'The Renault feels quick on the road, with few concessions needing to be made by the driver because of the diesel engine. Starting from cold is about the only time that the diesel really makes itself known.'

Motor magazine in August 1981 on the £5,595 18 TD.

The Renault 18 was France's riposte to the Cortina, a thoroughly modern 'conventional' four-door saloon.

to the front wheels, a bit unruly in slippery conditions.

Renault had a real hit on its hands, with well over 2 million 18s sold up to 1986. Its popularity extended well beyond Europe as the car was produced at ten different sites around the world. It was a worthy successor to the Renault 12 but, like that equally conventional but anonymous car, it's somewhat forgotten today.

The unusual alloy wheels, side rubbing strips and tail spoiler mark this one out as the 125bhp 18 Turbo.

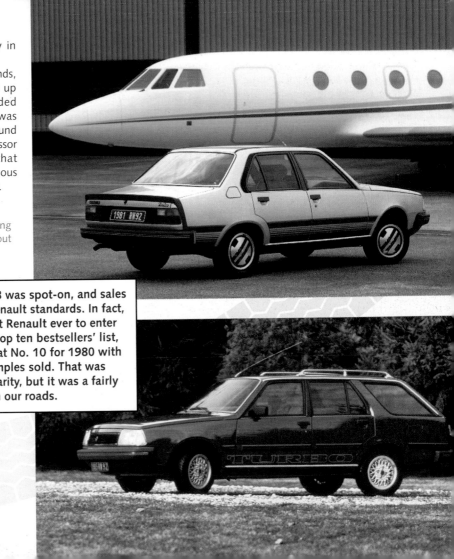

WHO LOVED IT?

For the Brits, the 18 was spot-on, and sales were huge by Renault standards. In fact, it was the first Renault ever to enter the British top ten bestsellers' list, slipping in at No. 10 for 1980 with 30,958 examples sold. That was its peak popularity, but it was a fairly common sight on our roads.

A Renault 18 estate with optional built-in roof rack bars; this and the saloon were briefly very popular in Britain.

Saab 900, 1978

In its several decades of existence – sadly, the marque went bankrupt in 2012 – Saab produced thoughtfully designed cars that made surprisingly good alternatives to mainstream models. With its 99 model of 1967, it forged a reputation for safety, quality and – after it added a turbocharger in 1977 – performance and prestige.

Trouble was, ranged against the resources of Mercedes-Benz, BMW and even our own Rover, Saab had to find ingenious ways to compete. And so it was when it came to replacing the much-loved 99.

Unable to afford a new car from the ground up, Saab instead used the existing passenger compartment of the 99, with its amazingly panoramic windscreen, and extended the wheelbase by 2in. To meet US crash laws, a longer nose was added, and an elongated tail section balanced it, creating a cavernous luggage space. With myriad other detail updates, the 900 was born, and went on sale in 1979.

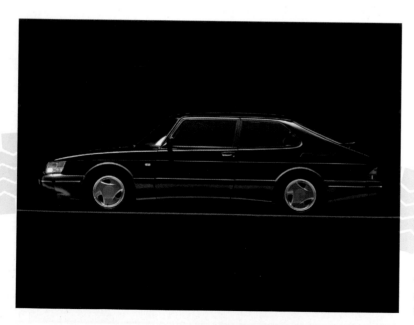

WHAT THEY SAID AT THE TIME

'When the turbo starts to take effect (at about 2,500rpm), it's stunning. There's an exhilarating surge of acceleration, amply demonstrated by the 50–70mph times in top.'

Motor magazine in October 1979 on the £9,910 900 Turbo three-door.

The worthy 900 became a potent executive express in turbo guise; notice the panoramic, wraparound windscreen.

The 900 Turbo was a cult performance car that cut it with the liveliest offerings from sporting makes like BMW and Alfa Romeo. This image broadened out the whole 900 range away from a few doctors, architects and other middle-class professionals and into the executive car mainstream.

WHO LOVED IT?

Saab did a marvellous job of turning its 900 into a spacious convertible, with chic looks and a brilliant quality soft-top.

With two-, three-, four- and five-door variations, and eventually a two-door convertible, there was plenty of bodystyle choice, but all 900s used incarnations of the same Saab 2.0-litre four-cylinder engine, driving the front wheels. The car's excellent, surefooted handling was truly exploited with the turbocharged engine option, reusing waste exhaust gases to boost engine power from 110bhp to 145bhp; that leapt to 175bhp when the engine went 16-valve in 1984.

All 900s offered extremely comfortable seats, logical controls,

and Saab-invented headlamp wipers. Their resistance to decay and owner abuse was a strong suit. Somehow, with the Vauxhall Cavalier-based range that replaced them in 1993, the unique 900 character was lost.

The four-door saloon version of the 900, here in Turbo form, still had folding rear seats for plenty of potential cargo space.

11

Mercedes-Benz S-Class, 1979

Those fastidious engineers at Mercedes' HQ in Stuttgart really pushed the boat out for this super-saloon. The all-new S-Class took a quantum leap forwards in terms of innovation, technology, power and style.

The star attraction among the car's line-up of features was the fitting, from 1981, of the world's first standard-equipment driver's airbag – this had been optional on a few American cars since the 1970s, but Mercedes' adoption of the life-saving technology began the process of making airbags standard equipment on every new car. Less significant but perhaps more useful in everyday driving were Merc's first polyurethane plastic bumpers.

The superb straight-six and all-alloy V8 engine range extended from 2.8 to 5.0 litres, so no S-Class was exactly a fuel-sipper. Manual transmission was available, but almost all these saloons and long-wheelbase limos came with the

WHO LOVED IT?

Every successful businessman the world over wanted an S-Class, and if things went extremely well then that's what he plumped for. The worlds of London showbiz and the diplomatic community sponged up the rest of an always restricted and fully priced British market allocation.

Mercedes had a few surprises to spring on the luxury car world with its S-Class, including concealed windscreen wipers.

excellent Mercedes-Benz four-speed automatic gearbox.

However, as part of the extremely sleek and well-proportioned styling, Merc added novel wind-cheating features like the world's first windscreen wipers that were concealed under the bonnet edge

From 1981, the S-Class became the first production car with a driver's airbag as standard, triggering an industry-wide trend.

when idle, and little aerofoils on the door handles. With a drag co-efficient of just 0.36, this big, wedge-shaped saloon was, briefly, the world's most aerodynamic production car, with wind noise in the already hushed interior cut to a minimum.

This S-Class remained the benchmark large luxury saloon of the 1980s, pretty much bar none. Little wonder, then, that these impressive cars were virtually depreciation-proof, such was the demand for them, although admittedly you had to be pretty loaded to afford one in the first place.

WHAT THEY SAID AT THE TIME

'Strong performance, positive power steering and surefooted handling mean it is still a fine driver's car but the low-speed ride and refinement fall slightly below the standards set by the Jaguar saloons.'

Motor magazine in October 1982 on the £18,800 380SE.

For such a large car, the S-Class was astonishingly aerodynamic, which helped to keep the interior free from wind and road noise.

Austin/MG Metro, 1980

Revealed on Friday, 8 October 1980, the Austin miniMetro made a huge and immediate impact, for it had been conceived against the depressing backdrop of British Leyland's toughest, bleakest years. The rapturous reception it received was a rare bright spot among the prevailing talk of strikes and factory closures.

British Leyland codenamed it LC8 while developing it in secret, but a 1979 poll of BL workers decided on the winning 'Metro' name. However, Birmingham train manufacturer Metro Cammell got wind of the choice, and insisted BL could only use the Metro name if prefixed with the 'mini' tag.

Some Metro aspects were the equal – if not better – of the rival Ford Fiesta, Renault 5 and Volkswagen Polo, particularly its interior space and nimble road manners. Several elements, though, were compromised because the drivetrain was borrowed from the 21-year-old Mini, giving a slightly awkward driving position, a whiny four-speed gearbox and a lack of mechanical refinement in the ageing A-Series engine.

Early TV commercials showed a battalion of Metros holding back European rivals from a vantage point above Dover's white cliffs. It

WHAT THEY SAID AT THE TIME

'In both cars, the motorway was easy meat. The 1.0-litre gave 80-plus, the 1.3 around 90mph. Overall I felt the Metro was almost happier at or beyond the legal speed limit than in "normal" conditions, no doubt thanks to the long gear ratios BL has chosen.'
London Evening Standard in October 1980 on the £3,095 Metro 1.0 and £3,995 Metro 1.3.

Austin Metros begin to pour off the Longbridge production lines in 1981 to satisfy huge demand across Britain.

This MG Metro Turbo could reach 110mph and accelerate like greased lightning, but a five-speed gearbox would have been appreciated.

Austin stole a match on the Ford Fiesta by cleverly squeezing two extra doors into the Metro, still within the standard wheelbase.

WHO LOVED IT?

The wide British motoring public seemed benevolently tolerant of the Metro's few drawbacks, and orders cascaded in. By June 1981 a newly minted Metro trundled out of the Longbridge factory every minute. By the end of the year it was Britain's No. 4 bestseller at 110,283, and it remained in the top five until 1988.

TV presenters Terry Wogan and Sue Cook auction off the millionth Metro made for the BBC's Children In Need charity.

was a blatantly patriotic statement that Prime Minister Margaret Thatcher surely approved of. One car magazine proclaimed: 'At last – a British car that no-one needs apologise for.' Hmm…

It was thrifty to run and maintain, and genuinely versatile with a cavernous hatchback and the novelty of an asymmetrically split folding rear seat. The car was fun to drive, too, and a 103mph 1275cc MG edition launched in 1982 capitalised on this … and came with natty pepper-pot alloy wheels, go-faster stripes and red seatbelts!

Fiat Panda, 1980

Fiat had one of its periodic bouts of design brilliance in 1980, when it allowed Giorgetto Giugiaro free rein to reinterpret the basic economy car for the 1980s. The family car styling maestro, with the acclaimed Alfasud, Golf and Audi 80 in his portfolio already, came up with a startlingly straight-lined, boxy shape for the Panda, with its all-round plastic body-cladding – for fending off city dings – and flat glass, even for the windscreen, to cut production costs and maximise interior space within its tight dimensions.

The four-seater interior was also an industrial designer's dream. The removable front seats could form a (fairly uncomfortable) bed, while the upholstery could be detached and chucked into the washing machine when it got grubby. There was a clip-on ashtray for the hammock-like front parcel shelf that stood in for a full-width dashboard, while the sun would blaze in through front and rear fabric roofs.

WHAT THEY SAID AT THE TIME

'Considered as basic motor car, and not as anything more ambitious, this new Fiat is distinctly clever in some ways, amusing and entertaining in others. Will it sell? How reluctant the British have always been in the past to buy basic cars!'

Autocar magazine in June 1981 on the £2,860 Panda 45.

Partly thanks to the flat glass panels in Giugiaro's utilitarian design, the Panda was a roomy little car.

WHO LOVED IT?

The original Panda is a design classic that served Europe well. In Britain, as elsewhere, it was affordable and useful as a utilitarian city runabout. We bought precisely 59,397 examples of the original Panda, which was but a small portion of the 4.5 million cars built.

Under the bonnet there were several engines to choose from. The early 650cc twin-cylinder, immensely popular back home in Italy, was never offered to UK customers, but the four-cylinder 903cc unit we did receive made the Panda a nippy buzzbox. A new range of Fiat's FIRE engines in 1986, a five-speed gearbox and an improved rear suspension set-up made the already-capacious Panda vastly more pleasant and less harsh to own.

The Panda's utilitarian cred was boosted in 1983 by the arrival of a version equipped with selectable four-wheel drive and raised ride height, and given another uplift with a tiny diesel engine option three years later.

Britain loved the Panda, snapping up almost 60,000 of them over a thirteen-year period; better engines used from 1986 made it even more likeable.

Ford Escort MkIII/Orion, 1980

Plenty of Fiesta engineering, especially front-wheel drive with a transversely mounted engine set-up, went into this brand new Escort, codenamed Project 'Erika' – either after a Ford manager's PA, or else as a reference to US Ford product planner Erick A. Reickert, depending on which story you believe.

Erika was a pan-European project combining the mechanical design skills from Ford of Britain's engineering centre at Dunton, Essex with the styling and body-engineering prowess from Ford of Europe at Merkenich in Germany.

Ford splashed £500 million on its new engine range, a project begun in 1974 and termed 'Compound Valve-angle, Hemispherical' (CVH). This new engine's efficiency was down to an alloy cylinder head with hemispherical combustion chamber – a classic layout but one that usually

WHAT THEY SAID AT THE TIME

'It responds readily to the helm and has secure road-holding on smooth, dry roads, cornering in an attitude of understeer which remains mild except through very tight corners.'

Motor magazine in March 1982 on the £5,276 Escort 1.3GL five-speed.

Right: The XR3 upheld the Escort tradition for stirring sports saloons, making do with twin carbs until the fuel-injected XR3i came on stream.

Left: Shown here in five-door Ghia form, the new Escort was a particularly neat family car with its 'bustle' rear end styling.

The boot space in the Escort-derived Orion saloon was simply enormous, despite having a high sill for loading.

WHO LOVED IT?

The MkIII Escort was simply the perfect car for the greatest number of British drivers. It enjoyed an unassailable position at the pinnacle of the British sales chart every single year between 1981 and 1989 – the whole of the 1980s, basically. With a major revamp in 1986 to keep the car fresh, it fully deserved its success.

required expensive twin camshafts to operate the valves. The 'compound valve-angle' element of the CVH meant Ford had cleverly located the valves so they could be operated by a single camshaft. There were versions in 1.1-, 1.3-, 1.4- and 1.6-litre sizes.

The styling, meanwhile, was also totally new: a tidy three- or five-door hatchback with a pronounced rear 'bustle' giving the shape an elegant balance and better high-speed stability. For this the Escort picked up a Design Council Award, and was also elected European Car of the Year for 1981.

Suspension used MacPherson struts front and back, but this was one area of the car panned by critics for its mediocre road-holding and ride quality.

Though the Escort was primarily a family car, Ford didn't ignore its loyal posse of performance addicts, and the XR3 version was pitched firmly at boy racers. First it had twin carburettors but soon gained fuel injection to become the revered XR3i, complete with wide alloy wheels and a multitude of spoilers. For the more traditional motorist, the Orion packed all the Escort's attributes in a traditional four-door saloon with a massive boot.

The Escort was immortalised by the Royal Mail in one of a series of 'then and now' postage stamps in 1982.

Vauxhall Astra, 1980

Every European car manufacturer worth its salt was taking a potshot at the pace-setting Volkswagen Golf in the late 1970s. Initially, few could match its all-round excellence, and the ranks of these second-raters included the Fiat Strada, Chrysler Horizon and Renault 14. But then along came Opel in 1979 with its D Series of Kadett, and all of a sudden its German rivals at Wolfsburg had something to worry about – not least because the new contender would undercut the Golf on price at most levels.

The car was totally new territory for the European branch of General Motors, being front-wheel drive with an all-new range of transverse, overhead-camshaft engines – whose lively performance came partly from their aluminium cylinder heads and hydraulic valve lifters.

The range included three- and five-door hatchbacks ('saloon' models with two or four doors and

WHAT THEY SAID AT THE TIME

'With the more potent 90bhp 1.6-litre Cavalier engine under its bonnet, the delightful Astra comes of age. With fine packaging, a slick gearchange and high standards of build and finish in its armoury, the Astra is still the car to beat.'

Motor magazine in January 1982 on the £5,507 Astra 1.6S GL three-door.

Left: It was not to everyone's taste, for sure, but the Astra GTE was the first to feature body coloured bumpers and wheels.

Above: The practical and efficient Astra (Opel Kadett in the rest of Europe) was the first family hatchback good enough to stand comparison to the all-conquering Golf.

a conventional bootlid in an identical profile were also briefly offered) and a five-door estate. Neat, rather than eye-catching, styling and a roomy cabin were keynotes.

Back in the late 1970s, British buyers faced the bizarre situation of being able to buy often near-identical Vauxhalls and Opels in the UK from separate dealers. And the Kadett was the first on sale here, followed five months later in February 1980 by Vauxhall's Astra edition, as a German-built import.

However, it took until November 1981 for British manufacture finally to get underway at Ellesmere Port in Cheshire, once it had stopped production of the extremely popular Chevette.

WHO LOVED IT?

From a cautious start, the Astra steadily built up a huge fanbase in the UK. The ever-critical buyer's guide *What Car?* declared it the best new car of 1980. After it became a proper 'British' car in 1981, this was assisted by the introduction of a superb diesel engine option, and then the Golf GTi-chasing, fuel-injected 1.8-litre Astra GTE – Britain's first car, incidentally, to feature an all-white livery including bumpers, mirrors and even wheels!

Vauxhall's Merseyside plant only started to build the Astra in 1981, with all cars up to that point imported from Germany.

Ford Capri 2.8 Injection, 1981

At the Geneva Motor Show in March 1981, there was a genuine surprise from Ford. The glory days of the old he-man Capri were thought to be long gone, killed off by hot hatchbacks, just as the first Capri itself had decimated two-seater sports car sales. Yet now it was fighting back with the 2.8 Injection. Ford had replaced the old 'Essex' 3.0-litre V6 engine with the 'Cologne' 2.8-litre V6, a much more modern design as used in the most upmarket Ford Granada. To this was added Bosch K-Jetronic fuel injection to produce 160bhp.

The car's chassis was comprehensively uprated to handle the potent new power unit. Lowered suspension was tuned and stiffened with thicker anti-roll bars and gas-filled shock absorbers, and the car rode on wide-rim Wolfrace 'pepper pot' alloy wheels fitted with Goodyear's 205/60VR NCT tyres. Front disc brakes were now ventilated. The centrepieces of the smartly trimmed interior were two snug Recaro sports seats.

It was good-looking, reliable, powerful, well equipped and easy

The Injection, like most Capris, was great fun to drive, and was made all the better when a five-speed gearbox was added.

WHAT THEY SAID AT THE TIME

'You always know exactly what's happening to the front wheels, which makes mid-corner steering corrections easy to apply. The power-assisted steering is quick and precise yet well weighted ... the seats are truly superb.'

Motor magazine in July 1982 on the £7,995 Capri 2.8 Injection.

The wide alloy wheels, with their 'pepper pot' design, were part of the upgrade package on the sparkling Capri 2.8 Injection.

WHO LOVED IT?

The 2.8 Injection's performance – with a 130mph top speed and 0–60mph sprint time of just 7.9 seconds – made it a match for the £16,732 Porsche 911SC – but at less than half that price tag. The Capri rendered both the temperamental £10,250 Alfa Romeo GTV6 and the portly £8,641 Datsun 280ZX irrelevant also-rans. It's a measure of the 2.8 Injection's huge British popularity that, of a grand total of around 25,000, fully 80 per cent went to buyers in Blighty.

to drive fast on twisty roads, perhaps with a touch of satisfyingly controllable oversteer where circumstances allowed.

It was even better to drive fast over long distances from January 1983 when it was gifted a five-speed gearbox, and grip was improved significantly in October 1984 with a limited-slip differential, when the car was subtly renamed the 2.8i S and given half-leather trim to match those Recaro seats. The 2.8i S had one of the shortest options lists of any Ford. The only extra-cost features on it were the choices of metallic or two-tone paintwork.

Greater Manchester Police was one force that employed high-speed Capri 2.8 Injections in its fight against crime.

Opel Manta, 1981

Just like the Ford Capri on the previous pages, the Manta was another sporty coupé whose heyday had been the 1970s. Actually, this was the Capri's closest rival, perhaps beating it on good looks but never quite touching it for macho image. Yet again, just like the Capri, the Manta gained a late-life boost with a clever makeover in 1981.

The MkII version of the car, essentially a coupé iteration of the Opel Ascona saloon, arrived in 1975, with engines available in this country ranging from 1.6 to 2.0 litres. There was a choice of a two-door coupé or three-door hatchback, and most versions had close equivalents in the very similar Vauxhall Cavalier range.

WHAT THEY SAID AT THE TIME

'A good driving position, excellent handling and a superb gearchange make it a fine driver's car. Ride comfort and ventilation could be better but it's still one of our favourites – especially at the keen price.'

Motor magazine in November 1982 on the £5,919 Manta Berlinetta 1.8S Coupé.

A well executed makeover, new engines and continuing success in tallying kept the Opel Manta fresh and relevant.

Handsome, fine-handling cars the lot of them, but with the arrival of front-wheel drive for the Ascona/Cavalier, time looked to be up for them. Not so. The new Ascona's efficient Family II range of engines were installed in these rear-drive cars, with overhead-camshafts, in 1.3, 1.8 and 2.0-litre sizes. Importantly, they could all run on unleaded petrol. Meanwhile, a cunning facelift left the metal unchanged but added new colour-matched bumpers, side skirts, grille, spoilers, graphics, trim and wheels.

There was real logic to extending the Manta's life. At the time, the rear-wheel drive Manta was covering Opel in glory thanks to its sterling performance in international rallying. So it proved a powerful magnet for pulling people into Vauxhall/Opel showrooms. However, by the time it was properly replaced by the Calibra in 1989, the old warhorse was definitely showing its age.

The Manta had always been a good-looking car, offering a great alternative to the Capri and also sold as part of the old Vauxhall Cavalier range.

WHO LOVED IT?

This was one of the last of its kind: a stylish, affordable, four-seater coupé with rear-wheel drive. It was easy to own and fun to throw around, and there was still a coterie of British traditionalists who wanted just such a combination.

Life on the Road in 1980s Britain

The completion of the M25 was the biggest road news of the decade. Prime Minister Margaret Thatcher cut the ribbon on 29 October 1986, in an opening ceremony between Junctions 22 for London Colney and 23 at South Mimms. She saluted Britain's road-building skills and explained how already-opened sections were slashing journey times and freeing villages from lorry tyranny.

In her address, Mrs Thatcher likened motorways to supermarkets. 'The saying is: "Nobody shops at Sainsbury's because of the queues",' she said. 'Its popularity is a mark of its success, not of its failure.'

Measuring just over 117 miles, the M25 became the world's longest circular city bypass, or orbital road (although now outdone by Germany, wouldn't you just know it, with its 122-mile A10 loop around Berlin), with the clockwise off-slip at Reigate the longest sliproad anywhere outside the USA.

Massive growth in car ownership in suburban London forced 1960s road planners to devise a 'Ringway'

With the opening of the complete M25 in 1986, Britain entered the joined-up era of multi-lane highway travel; here a traffic policeman keeps motorway watch with his Rover 800 patrol car.

Most of the outlying parts of the UK mainland were linked up to the motorway network by the start of the 1980s, although drivers faced plenty of inconvenience when things went wrong.

motorway plan: Ringway 1 would be an inner-London 'traffic box', Ringway 2 the North and South Circular Roads, Ringway 3 an inner suburban motorway, and Ringway 4 an outer rural motorway.

Constructing the very first part of what became the M25 began in 1973, today the stretch between Junctions 23 and 24 for South Mimms and Potters Bar.

Back then, this initial section of Ringway 4 was named M16 when it opened in September 1975. A year later, the bulldozers initiated Ringway 3 between Dartford and Swanley in Kent, set to be called M25.

Yet the ultimate M25 is actually two planned motorways squeezed together. In November 1975, the expansive Ringways plan was axed on cost and planning

Between 1980 and 1990, the number of registered vehicles increased by about a fifth, putting added pressure on UK road space.

grounds. The part of Ringway 4 that, on today's M25, forms the J5–19 section was joined up with the northern and eastern sections of Ringway 3, forming the Surrey-distended circle familiar today.

Isolated stretches were laid down – only 19 miles was completed by 1980 – and then gradually linked up and opened until the entire route was finished: the three final parts to open in 1986 were the sections J19–23, J1A–2, and J3–5. The M16 title was junked, and the whole motorway gained the M25 name. It took eleven years to build, costing £909 million – £7.5 million per mile. The mammoth project used 3.5 million tonnes of asphalt for its surface, topping 2 million tonnes of concrete.

Pent-up demand for a way to navigate the south-east without entering the capital city was massive ... and the M25 proved inadequate from day one! By 1993, 200,000 vehicles were daily using a motorway space designed for 88,000, so the first major modification in October 1989 was an extra lane added between Junctions 11 and 13.

A typical example of a 1980s contraflow: the inevitable logjam that built up whenever urgent road repairs were needed.

Capital Radio's 'Mile Muncher', a Ford Transit advertising the London commercial station, circled the newly completed M25 motorway continuously for seven days and nights in 1986.

Towns and villages around London's outer perimeter were supposed to be helped by the M25, relieving them of heavy transitory traffic and turning their high streets tranquil again.

There was only one motorway services, at South Mimms, until 1992. The M25's biggest ever fatal pile-up had occurred in December 1984, well before the whole thing was even opened; nine people died as twenty-six vehicles collided in dense fog that descended suddenly near Godstone. In August 1988 a 22-mile traffic jam formed between Junctions 8 and 9, a record-holder until 1995.

Little wonder husky-voiced rock guitarist Chris Rea entitled the song (and album) that it inspired *The Road to Hell*. It was released in 1989.

The M25's problems, of course, stand small beside the tremendous cost and time saving it delivered to millions. Anyone driving around the UK in the early 1980s was acutely aware of the benefits motorways brought.

In 1980, for instance, Scottish drivers saw the completion of two important motorways that hugely enhanced the road network there. The final sections were now in place of both the M8 linking Scotland's two major urban centres of Glasgow and Edinburgh, and the M90 between the Forth Road Bridge and Perth.

This was also the year when the M11, as it exists today, was finally ready to receive traffic, helping road access to England's outlying eastern region.

Many key 'A' roads around the country were expanded with dual carriageway sections, the A13 in Essex one of many boosted in such a way to accommodate more intensive use. In 1989, the government also announced plans to upgrade the entire north–south A1 'Great North Road' to motorway status, although this scheme was formally abandoned by 1995.

The number of vehicles on the country's roads was swelling inexorably. In 1980, there were 19.2 million registered, and by the end of 1989 there were 24.2 million – a spurt of one fifth. As the key 20 million level was only breached in 1983, clearly the fastest growth came in the second half of the '80s.

Major road bridges were another way to help drivers get where they wanted to more quickly. Possibly the most impressive was the Humber Bridge, a 1.5-mile wonder of suspension technology – with the world's longest single span (today relegated to being the seventh longest) – linking what had been Yorkshire and Lincolnshire but now helping to unify

Motorcyclist, Allegro, Marina and a Datsun Bluebird jostle for position as a policeman stands in to direct traffic at a 1970s trouble spot.

The Humber Bridge opened in 1981; it cost £28 million to build and has never recouped its cost, but the people of Lincolnshire and Yorkshire value it as a vital link in an otherwise laborious to negotiate riverside region.

Humberside. It opened in June 1981 amid controversy that its go-ahead was politically motivated rather than of genuine benefit, as it's always seen light use relative to its hefty £28 million estimated construction cost. Tolls to use it have never come close to repaying its debt burden.

That cannot be said for the Queen Elizabeth II road bridge at Dartford, which feeds so much cash into the Treasury that plans to scrap tolls once its build cost had been repaid have been torn up.

Even before the M25 reached both ends of the Dartford Tunnel between Kent and Essex, planners knew it could never cope with the motorway's unrelenting traffic volumes, so they bored a second tunnel, costing £45 million and opened in 1980. But even that was insufficient, so the bridge to boost capacity at the M25's Dartford River Crossing was approved in 1986, and work started in August 1988. The Queen opened the four-lane, cable-stayed bridge in October 1991 – the first new bridge of any sort spanning the River Thames in fifty years – and it's fed traffic south (the twin tunnels look after the northbound onslaught) ever since.

How safe were Britain's roads in the 1980s? Well, your chances of being killed in a car crash were certainly diminishing, albeit slowly. In 1980, 6,010 people died in road accidents; by 1983 it was down to 5,445; by 1986 it was 5,382; and in 1989 the annual figure stood at 5,373.

One of the key factors behind these falling stats set against rising vehicle ownership and use was seatbelts. On 31 January 1983, wearing front seatbelts, where the car had them (and every new one sold since 1967 did), became compulsory. It had taken ten years for the proposal to enter law as the legislation shuffled slowly through parliamentary process.

Instantly, and despite grumblings about civil liberties being infringed, 90 per cent of drivers and front seat passengers complied; there was an immediate and dramatic fall in serious injuries sustained in non-fatal traffic accidents. From 1987, standard fitment of rear seatbelts was introduced; three years later, all children under the age of 14 had to wear them if they were there, and four years later that applied to adults too.

Although road safety initiatives appeared to move at a glacial pace during the 1980s, major efforts were afoot to improve things. In 1984, for example, a Europe-wide harmonisation programme set many safety-related

In 1983, and after nearly a decade of political debate and obfuscation, the wearing of front seatbelts finally became a legal requirement.

Harmonisation with Europe initiated many safety benefits, such as the requirement that car tyres need at least 1.6mm of tread depth to be considered safe.

The German car industry led the way on car safety systems in the 1980s; here Mercedes-Benz test drivers compare S-Class cars with and without anti-lock brakes.

minimum standards, including issues like a 50mg blood alcohol maximum limit for drink-driving, and a minimum tread depth of 1.6mm for tyres to be deemed roadworthy. Later, 1986 was declared European Road Safety Year as a demonstration of even more intent, and led to the founding of the AA Foundation for Road Safety Research.

In 1982, the new 'totting-up' system of driving licence penalties was introduced, with more than twelve points leading to an automatic driving ban. It was an effective way to tackle both recklessness and simple carelessness. But further measures to tame errant drivers were arriving thick and fast. In 1986, London's Chelsea, Kensington and Westminster saw the arrival of wheel clamps to deter selfish parkers; these yellow steel horrors were briefly known as 'Denver boots' after their American place of origin, and caused fury among 'victims'.

And then, in 1988, Nottingham saw the first spy cameras installed to snap motorists who ran red lights, beginning the blanket camera surveillance epidemic so familiar on the national roadscape today. The era of 'Big Brother' had been forecast in George Orwell's novel *1984*; now, just four years later than he predicted, it had actually arrived for Britain's indignant drivers.

By 1988, cameras were being installed to record drivers who disregarded the rules of the road, such as stopping at a red light.

Triumph Acclaim, 1981

The terrible financial plight of British Leyland couldn't have escaped your notice in the late '70s and early '80s. The company had been nationalised to save it from bankruptcy in 1975 and henceforth the struggle to make it viable again frequently saw workers and management at loggerheads.

Understandably, there was little spare cash sloshing around to create new models, and most resources were poured into the Metro. Larger cars had to be postponed but, in the meantime, the dealers required something decent to sell, as the ancient Allegro, Ital, Maxi and Dolomite were in steep decline.

Honda threw a lifeline. On Boxing Day in 1979, feisty BL chief Michael Edwardes signed an agreement with the Japanese firm for Project Bounty. This was a licence to produce the

WHAT THEY SAID AT THE TIME

'Triumph's Acclaim is really of Honda stock, though with peppy performance, excellent economy and a fine ride/handling compromise as family traits, that's no bad thing. A capable all-rounder with a bright future.'

Motor magazine in October 1981 on the £4,688 Acclaim HL.

British Leyland lucked out by choosing Honda as a partner, which provided the Civic-based Acclaim model as a lifeline.

Honda Ballade, a four-door saloon version of the well-liked Civic, in the UK, and as the Triumph Acclaim it became the first Japanese car to be built in Europe.

To qualify as 'British', some 70 per cent of its components, by value, were sourced here, with the main foreign imports from Japan being the all-aluminium 1.3-litre overhead-camshaft engine and five-speed gearbox. Nonetheless, Japanese cars were feared and loathed by European manufacturers, and Italy in particular tried hard to dispute the Acclaim's British credentials, but eventually conceded.

British Leyland fine-tuned the Acclaim's suspension to suit British roads, and tried to make the rather cramped interior more accommodating for the typical local driver by re-designing the seats. In all other respects this new car was already spot-on. Far from simply fort-holding until the Maestro arrived in 1983, the compact four-door saloon became an essential element of the BL range.

Acclaim body shells about to enter the assembly process at Cowley; the little saloon had a very good reputation for quality.

WHO LOVED IT?

Here was the small saloon with light controls, a responsive nature, great refinement and excellent build quality that suburban Britain was crying out for. With just 70bhp, it was no sports car, but many of the older drivers who bought one weren't concerned about that. In 1982 and '83 it was a top ten bestseller, and a creditable 133,000 examples were sold.

Vauxhall Cavalier MkII, 1981

The Cavalier name became a British roadscape staple over its twenty on-sale years, its three generations and its mightily impressive 1.7 million sales.

The car you see is the second version and although the original Cavalier did well enough for Vauxhall, this replacement really lit the blue touch paper for the marque. Without doubt it was *the* car that made Britain finally take Vauxhall seriously. So just why was it so successful?

WHAT THEY SAID AT THE TIME

'The excellent all-round capabilities of the Vauxhall Cavalier, and its lack of any significant deficiencies, place it firmly in first place among fleet market contenders – the outright winner.'

Motor magazine in January 1982 on the £5,814 Cavalier 1.6GL.

WHO LOVED IT?

In 1984 and '85, the Cavalier was the country's second bestselling car after the Ford Escort, an unprecedented feat for General Motors' outpost here. It was a huge favourite with mid-range company car drivers, motorway-pounding sales reps, and came in a wide variety of versions from austere 1.3-litre to 120mph 2.0-litre SRi, to match all pay grades.

The four-door saloon of the all-new Cavalier was the version that most appealed to former Cortina owners seeking something more contemporary.

A scene from a great TV ad to launch the fuel-injected Cavalier in 1983, showing it flying high above all its opponents.

There are three factors. First, it switched from rear- to front-wheel drive, and everyone who drove it was immediately impressed by its sound road-holding, safe handling and excellent chassis design; power steering was only fitted on the luxury CDi, but it wasn't an issue – the others didn't really need it to still be manoeuvrable at parking speeds.

Second, the Ford Sierra, launched in 1982, dismayed many because of its dated rear-wheel drive driveline carried over wholesale from the departing Cortina. Many more deeply disliked its 'jelly mould' styling. Former Ford loyalists defected to the Cavalier in droves, especially for its terrific diesel engine.

And third, the Cavalier came as a four-door saloon and five-door hatch from day one – a more popular line-up than the Sierra's early hatch-or-estate choice (a Cavalier estate was added later, and sold poorly, while a short-lived Cavalier convertible barely sold at all).

The Cavalier deserved every ounce of its huge popularity. This 'J-Car' design was sold worldwide under eight other General Motors brands, even including Cadillac – the most ever for one single car design.

Volkswagen Polo MkII, 1981

It's fair to say this Polo elicited little genuine excitement when it was new, and you wouldn't exactly cross the road to drool over one now, more than three decades on. Nonetheless, for anyone who picked one over a Metro, Fiesta or Renault 5, the choice was wise. Just as for the outgoing model, the new Polo was built with typical German care and solidity, and the quality of its mechanical parts ensured the cars would give lengthy, dependable service with the minimum of attention.

Unveiled in autumn 1981 and in showrooms across Britain the following spring, Volkswagen designers had taken a pragmatic approach to shaping the car. The squared-off rear end was more like an estate car than a hatchback, making it a brilliant cargo-swallower for its compact overall dimensions. The so-called Coupé model, introduced in 1983, was more like a conventional supermini; there was also a conservative-looking two-door saloon, the Polo Classic.

The 1.0- or 1.3-litre engines gave economy and sprightliness respectively, and five years after launch they were uprated with hydraulic tappets, new camshafts and valve gear, plus an automatic choke. With a stylistic makeover along the way, these Volkswagens soldiered on until 1994.

The MkII was launched in an era of economic recession, rising fuel

WHAT THEY SAID AT THE TIME

'It's a well-made and spacious car with a crisp gear-change, taut handling and a comfortable driving position. Its heating, ventilation, finish, visibility and instruments are all among the best on offer in the supermini class. On the debit side are its brakes and ride comfort.'

Motor magazine in January 1982 on the £4,574 Polo 1.1 GL.

The second-generation Polo in its mainstream form was something of a pint-sized estate car, with van-like cargo space.

WHO LOVED IT?

For just a little bit more than the cost of an 'ordinary' car, you could have this thrifty and versatile VW, and it proved a big seller in the UK among middle-class motorists spending their own money, or as a second car. Its values were reflected in buoyant second-hand values.

With a conventional boot in a 'three box' shape, the saloon model was labelled the Polo Classic, giving buyers plenty of variety.

prices and renewed pressure to cut emissions. So VW used it as a testbed for its new Formel E technology. This fuel-efficient package arrived as an option in 1983. The transmission had a high gear ratio for lower revs, the 1.3-litre engine was a high-compression unit, and it came with a then very novel stop-start system that cut the engine when the car was idle for more than two seconds, such as when stationary in traffic. The last was a portent of what we enjoy widely today, but Formel E was actually dropped in 1986.

Although it looks like a normal hatchback, VW called this one the Polo Coupé, which really it was beside the boxy standard model.

Citroën BX, 1982

Citroën's history is peppered with a galaxy of landmark models such as the Traction Avant, 2CV and DS but, although routinely overlooked these days, the BX is also an extremely significant model.

It took the best of the technical avant-garde for which the French marque had become justly renowned – some might even say notorious – and massaged it into a reasonably 'normal' family car offering space and performance that could equal and perhaps better anything from Ford or Volkswagen.

The BX was built on an entirely new platform that incorporated hydropneumatic suspension and powered disc brakes; marque traditionalists must also have approved of the characteristically Citroën single-spoke steering wheel and secondary controls operated by switches on dashboard-mounted drums rather than on the more usual stalks.

Indeed, this was the first ever corporate model developed by the Peugeot group which made its debut as a Citroën; the Bertone-styled BX formed the basis of the Pininfarina-penned Peugeot 405 five years later. So, of course, it featured Peugeot 1.3- and 1.6-litre engines from the start, while for certain markets there was in addition a frugal, if

WHAT THEY SAID AT THE TIME

'Despite its relatively modest power output, it does a lot with its generous spread of torque, Citroën obviously reasoning that with a slippery shape (Cd: 0.34) and only moderately long gearing, solid bottom and mid-range punch would give the best performance/economy compromise. The figures say they were right.'

Motor magazine in September 1984 on the £6,313 BX 19RD.

Citroën's hydropneumatic suspension made the BX estate an especially stable and spacious load-lugger.

A plastic bonnet and tailgate, in addition to bumper sections, helped shave weight from the futuristic Citroën BX.

gutless, 1.1. Beginning in 1984, the company's excellent diesel and later turbo diesel units were offered, while the GTi could boast France's first-ever 16-valve engine.

There were some other innovations, too. The BX was among the first family saloons to offer the option of four-wheel drive, while the car broke new ground in its use of weight-saving plastic for the bodywork, having a glass-fibre bonnet, hatch-back and bumpers.

> **WHO LOVED IT?**
>
> This was an uncommonly successful car for Citroën in Britain, probably making big sales gains from people unhappy with various facets of Ford's new Sierra. As well as highly competitive pricing, Citroën also got its fleet sales operation working hard, so many BXs were run as company cars.

With the optional four-wheel drive, the BX became a firm favourite with Britain's legions of caravanners.

Ford Sierra, 1982

The introduction of the Sierra was one of the most anticipated, and most controversial, in British motoring history. The reason for the near-hysteria was that the car would supplant the venerable Cortina, the automotive equivalent of an old pair of slippers with which two generations of the country's drivers had become entirely comfortable.

Although always carefully, some might say cynically, designed, none of the four generations of Cortina had ever been close to technology's cutting edge. So for its replacement, Ford elected to play safe on the mechanicals and go adventurous on the styling.

Its designers created a startlingly different profile with a curvaceous, wind-cheating shape and, just like the recent Escort, a bustle-backed rear end incorporating a hatchback. Along with prominent plastic bumpers and a boldly shaped, ergonomic interior, the car provoked more shock than awe; 'jelly mould' was the most frequent derogatory brickbat lobbed at it.

Shock of the new: the radical new profile for Ford's crucial large family car polarised opinion, many declaring it a 'jelly mould'.

'Super-smooth 2.3 V6 makes for very civilised progress while slippery shape and long gearing, with the optional five-speed, help economy. Outstanding ride/handling compromise, comfortable driving position are other virtues.'

Motor magazine in December 1982 on the £8,567 Sierra 2.3 Ghia.

The XR4i, packing a 2.8-litre V6 engine, uses the Space Shuttle as a pointer to its aerodynamic prowess.

Yet, just below the surface and except for a new independent rear suspension system, it was little removed from the rear-drive Cortina 80. Four-cylinder engine choice ranged from 1.3 to 2.0 litres, with a 2.3 V6 and a coarse Peugeot-supplied 2.3 diesel. A 2.8-litre V6 powered the sporty XR4i and the later 150mph RS Cosworth had a fire-breathing turbocharged 2.0-litre, both cars displaying spectacular rear spoilers fully in keeping with the Sierra's 'aero' looks. There were four-wheel drive and estate variants too.

Ford had decreed hatchbacks were the way forward, but in 1987 bowed to market pressure for traditional four-door saloons with the Sierra Sapphire. It was the ultimate 'normalising' of this once polarising product, but the Sierra's modernity meant it aged pretty well, and lasted until 1993.

WHO LOVED IT?

Not the British press, and nor either a large part of the Cortina-driving masses. Unlike its predecessor, the Sierra never topped the sales charts, although it must be said that popular taste swung anyway to smaller models. But after a shaky start, the Sierra settled into its place as a popular member of the Ford line-up.

Suzuki SJ, 1982

Here we are at the very beginnings of 'lifestyle' four-wheel drive with one of the true market pioneers. Industry minnow (at the time) Suzuki dipped its toe in the water with the dinky SJ and soon found quite a goodly number of people fancied one of these low-powered 4x4s as an everyday vehicle. And that many of them – surprise, surprise – would never tackle a rutted farm track, muddy fields or hazardous construction sites.

Not, it should be said, that the SJ made a very good town car. It was designed as a rugged working vehicle, with a separate chassis and unbreakable leaf-spring suspension all-round, so ride comfort was of secondary importance to off-road ability where, with its high approach and departure angles, it was a nimble little rock-hopper. Gas-filled shock absorbers did their best to add a little cushioning. Four-wheel drive was selectable so, on tarmac, top speed could be a deafening 75mph and hitting 60mph from a standstill took a good twenty seconds.

Power for the SJ410 came from a 45bhp 1.0-litre four-cylinder petrol engine, and there was a more powerful 1.3 in the later SJ413. Body styles offered included van, long-wheelbase pick-up, estate and – the number one choice for the unabashed poseur – a soft-top.

WHAT THEY SAID AT THE TIME

'The little Suzukis have to be taken seriously off-road, with a power-to-weight ratio second only to a Land Rover, and axle articulation on a par with the best. I slid my way down the slope without traumas, and bounced my way over to the hill'

Autocar magazine in March 1986 on the £4,999 SJ410 Hardtop.

Suzuki's dinky little SJ, here in late-model Samurai Sport form, jumped the species divide to deliver 'lifestyle' four-wheel drive to the suburban masses.

WHO LOVED IT?

It was customary to see big hair, big sunglasses, fake tan and a white jumpsuit behind the steering wheel, and just occasionally a weathered face and Barbour jacket. The SJ was very popular in the UK; so much so that Suzuki even arranged for production to begin in Spain so unrestricted import sales of a 'European' model could satisfy demand.

Some SJs might have been driven by Billericay beauty therapists, but the little vehicle could certainly cut it off-road, as its maker intended.

The SJ quickly became a cult vehicle, and was the first Suzuki car, as opposed to motorbike, to sell in large numbers in export markets outside Japan. As a rural runabout for those with logs and Labradors to focus on, it actually made a huge amount of sense, because running costs were vastly less than for a Land Rover.

Two proud Suzuki executives pose with the 500,000th example of SJ, which had become a cult hit all over the world.

Talbot Samba, 1981

This supermini did its best to breathe some life into the ailing Talbot marque. Front-wheel drive and with a choice of three engines from 1.0 to 1.3 litres, it also came as an attractive two-door, four-seater convertible – called a Cabriolet, and built by coachbuilder Pininfarina – with a built-in roll bar that made it a cut-price alternative to a soft-top Golf.

The car was actually a modified Peugeot 104 three-door and, although they look superficially the same, the only shared panels were the tailgate and bonnet; new grille, black window surrounds and Talbot livery were further differentiators.

A 1.3-litre Samba with five-speed gearbox was quite a lively, crisp-handling car to drive, while the 1124cc-engined Samba GL was, briefly, Europe's most economical production car, with 61mpg possible for feather-footed drivers.

Sambas were on sale for a mere four years between 1982 and 1986. It was at this point that the Talbot name for cars was consigned once more to history. It had been revived in 1979 after Peugeot paid a token

WHO LOVED IT?

Just shy of 200,000 Sambas were sold, 13,000 of which were Cabriolets, and a reasonable number came to the UK (the cars were built in Paris). But Talbot had the whiff of failure to it even as the Samba went on sale, and Peugeot's own 205 was a far superior vehicle, so the omens were never great.

Without doubt the most alluring of all the Sambas was the Cabriolet, designed and built by Pininfarina.

The Samba – this is the austere LS model – was based wholesale on the Peugeot 104 Coupé, and none the worse for that, either.

WHAT THEY SAID AT THE TIME

'Talbot's keenly priced new baby has excellent economy and is an exceptionally refined motorway cruiser. Easy to drive thanks to smooth, light controls. Small boot and limited legroom are disappointing features.'

Motor magazine in February 1982 on the £4,017 Samba GL.

$1 to take on Chrysler's ailing European operations. But sticking the badge (whose tangled British roots went back to the car-making venture of the Earl of Shrewsbury & Talbot in 1903) on Chrysler cars did not result in an upturn in fortunes, and Peugeot decided to axe the parallel range and concentrate on its core marque. In truth, the Samba was just about the best new car Talbot ever came up with; and there were only two of them, the other being the Tagora, an utter lemon of an executive saloon.

A little bit of sparkle was added to the Samba for the peppy S model, but the days of the Talbot marque were numbered.

Volkswagen Scirocco MkII, 1982

Since 1974 the Scirocco had been offering a sophisticated, front-wheel drive alternative to the Capri, Manta and Toyota Celica – an extremely good-looking four-seater coupé with all the excellent mechanical attributes of the Golf. There was a price premium to be paid, of course, but only a relatively restricted supply of these cars had held sales back.

In replacing the much-loved original with this new model, Volkswagen arguably sacrificed the Scirocco's sharp-edged, urbane character – the work of Italian design maestro Giorgetto Giugiaro – and replaced it with an aerodynamic but rather anonymous style, created by in-house designers.

VW engineers also changed the car's character by softening the ride, and so blunting the sporting edge of its otherwise very good handling. And under the new clothes the car still used a Golf MkI floorpan, meaning it would begin to feel slightly behind the times sooner rather than later.

But these were minor grumbles. It was typically well built, in this case by VW's famous collaborator Karmann, and in GTI form there was plenty of go from the 110bhp, fuel-injected engine, while the 90bhp GT was at least spritely.

There was a decent rear tailgate and the back seats could be folded, although the sill to get heavy suitcases in was quite high. The car was noteworthy for the time in offering standard rear seatbelts, and the tailgate glass curved down below waist level, although the Scirocco's

WHAT THEY SAID AT THE TIME

'Well finished and equipped but relatively poor value compared with the Golf GTi. Good performance and economy coupled with precise handling and a slick gearchange.'

Motor magazine in February 1982 on the £7,125 Scirocco GTi.

pretty average all-round visibility wasn't helped by the plastic spoiler positioned across it. However, it was part of the car's wind-cheating package that made the Scirocco notably light on petrol.

There was something a little less sharp-suited about the new Scirocco over the old one, but it was very much up to date aerodynamically.

This Scirocco GTX with 16-valve engine was one of the sportiest models in the new range; the cars were on sale until 1992.

WHO LOVED IT?

While rival coupés were growing old and withered on the vine, the new Scirocco was bursting with contemporary style and modern road manners. It sold strongly in the UK in a variety of versions, including the Storm with an all-leather interior.

Volvo 760, 1982

Just when everyone thought Volvos could hardly get any more square-rigged and hefty, the Swedes shocked the car world with the 760, a saloon that looked like it had been shaped with a ruler and set square and chiselled from solid steel.

Actually, it was 100kg lighter than the equivalent 240 model, and thanks to a wheelbase stretched by 10cm the road-holding was considerably improved, although a traditional live axle for the rear-wheel drive system was old-fashioned, no matter how robust it made the car. The older 264 was the source for most of the mechanical hardware. Under the bonnet was a 2.8-litre V6, so there was plenty of power, while a 2.0-litre petrol turbo and a 2.4 turbo diesel were added later, as was the less luxurious 740 model in saloon and vastly capacious estate editions. With the turbo diesel, it was the world's fastest accelerating car of its type.

Volvo had been working away on the 760's design since 1975, trying to find a way to reverse the company's sliding fortunes in a rocky world economy. So the 760, especially in top-notch GLE form, was intended to take the marque upmarket – an opulent new Volvo to rival Mercs, Rovers, BMWs and Jags. Several designs were considered, but the eventual straight-edged style, with a near-vertical rear window, would lower manufacturing costs … and it just happened to score very well in American consumer clinic surveys. Plus, it made for a very roomy interior, with air-conditioning, a sunroof and power steering as standard.

WHAT THEY SAID AT THE TIME

'Forget about the styling, Volvo's 760 GLE flagship really is good, with brisk performance, reasonable economy and fine handling. It's also refined, roomy and nicely finished. In short, it's the best car Volvo have ever made.'

Motor magazine in January 1983 on the £12,598 760 GLE automatic.

Some people deplored the slabby styling of the 760 yet critics rated the car as the best Volvo ever for performance, handling and roominess.

WHO LOVED IT?

After a few doubts over the drastic new profile, Britain's legions of Volvo owners took to the 700 Series, especially the 740 estate which had huge appeal to antique dealers and country types seeking a safe and comfortable hauler. In all, over 1.2 million of the cars were made up to 1990, about a fifth of them the opulent 760, and Britain remained one of Volvo's most important territories.

STAGE DOOR

The 740 Estate was probably the most popular of the 700 Series Volvos in Britain, with its massive capacity for swallowing cargo.

Audi 100, 1983

This is the car that really embedded aerodynamics in the conscience of consumers as an essential element of efficiency. In a project driven by innovation obsessive Ferdinand Piëch, Audi's chief engineer, the all-new Audi executive car boasted the lowest co-efficient of drag – the equation-result measure of wind-cheating ability – of any production car in the world. At 0.30, it was more slippery even than the overtly 'aero' Ford Sierra.

The smooth overall shape was assisted by the world-first use of flush-fitting side windows, and close attention to the way air was sucked around the engine bay and underneath, where the unseen floorpan was carefully shaped for optimum flow.

The 'Cd 0.30' badge of honour was worn as a decal in the rear quarter light, although it should be said that it applied only to the base model with narrow tyres and flush wheel trims. The car was also lighter than rivals, with even its jack being made from aluminium instead of steel.

As a result, Audi fitted relatively small engines, at first a 1.8 four-cylinder and 2.2 five-cylinder petrol, and later a 2.0 five-cylinder turbo diesel in a car that was the first to wear the now ubiquitous TDI label. In such an efficient car, they gave an excellent performance, with a top speed of 134mph possible, coupled with excellent fuel economy. A sister model called the 200 came with turbocharging and four-wheel drive, and in 1985 broke more new ground by becoming the first mass-market car with a completely galvanised body shell.

Here's what all the fuss was about: the 100 in a wind tunnel to demonstrate its leading co-efficient of drag of a mere 0.30.

WHAT THEY SAID AT THE TIME

'It combines a very high top speed with exceptional economy. The long gearing that helps achieve this minimal thirst is paid for with very poor top gear flexibility, but motorway cruising is serene.'

Motor magazine in February 1983 on the £10,996 100 CD.

WHO LOVED IT?

Audi had a hit on its hands and a potent new weapon in its developing battle with home-turf rivals BMW and Mercedes-Benz. With the new 100's launch, we first heard Audi's slogan of 'Vorsprung durch technik', coined by Audi's British advertising agency and memorably uttered by actor Geoffrey Palmer in the TV ad with the adjunct '…as they say in Germany'. It was soon adopted globally.

It may have looked big and impressive but the highly efficient Audi 100 called for relatively small engines to give it excellent performance.

Keeping Your Car Going in the 1980s

Mainstream 1980s cars now seem to represent something of a golden era. A lively discussion around the question 'Were 1980s cars more reliable?' on the Honest John website, one of Britain's most popular online motoring forums, debated some of the factors.

Most of the (generally older) drivers posting claimed that cars of the early part of the decade were very straightforward to maintain compared with those emerging at the end. One said: '1980s diesels were really simple and straightforward affairs, and very reliable, 'cos they didn't have all the electric guff which gives grief.'

'My 1982 2.8 Granada runs like clockwork,' said another. 'It's very easy to work on due to space around the engine. If I look under the bonnet of my 2003 [Vauxhall] Astra 2.0dti, the engine looks shoehorned in and I wouldn't be able to get a mini socket set anywhere near it!'

A regular oil change would do wonders for the typical 1980s car that was so much more reliable than its predecessors and yet not too complex to make opening the bonnet scary.

A Ford Granada rigged up to testing equipment in the laboratory to test emissions; from the 1980s all cars would need to spew out substantially less pollution.

Fitting catalytic converters to car exhaust systems, as standard equipment or to vehicles already in use, filtered out much in the way of noxious emissions. But unleaded petrol was essential.

Unleaded fuel would become widespread as the car industry cleaned up its act. It went on sale in 1986 but, by the end of that year, it was still offered at just eleven forecourts.

Britain's petrol stations were evolving, with the diesel pump now brought in from the cold under the canopy as sales of diesel cars soared, unleaded going nationwide, and the range of goodies on sale in the adjacent forecourt shops growing ever wider.

Others acknowledged that, alongside cars from the pre-1980s era, durability had improved dramatically. One wistfully recalled driving back and forth to Germany in a Mini in the early 1960s, praising its mechanical stamina ... but admitting he had to spend several evenings a week adjusting and renewing things on the car. Another recalled how, in previous times, engines that lasted 80–100,000 miles were regarded as remarkable exceptions. 'It's easy to forget just how much regular maintenance cars needed then,' he said. 'Gapping and replacing points, renewing rotor arms and condensers, re-setting the timing and adjusting the mixture were the stuff of life for a car owner.'

So the typical car of the early 1980s was better made than ever before, yet still basic enough to be easily maintained. We now know, though, that the situation would quickly change: cars would start to get much more complicated.

Motor vehicles were causing increasingly unacceptable levels of pollution, and governments were using legislation to force them to clean up. Germany blazed the trail in 1985, where tax incentives spurred on sales of cars equipped with catalytic converters. These complex filters on the exhaust system reduced emissions of harmful waste gases – specifically carbon monoxide (which hinders breathing and impairs co-ordination, especially in children), nitrogen oxide (which contributes to acid rain and ozone) and volatile organic compounds (which increase ozone formation) – by 90 per cent.

'Cats', however, are ruined by petrol containing lead, so a new grade of unleaded fuel was needed. By the end of 1986, this was on sale in Britain, although at that

Halfords, like other British retailers, was opening huge stores in out-of-town retail parks. A sign of the times in the economically squeezed early '80s was this petrol-saving guide they gave away free at their ever busier tills.

time it was only available at eleven forecourts, and cost 4.6p more per gallon than four-star.

From a slow start, unleaded petrol quickly went nationwide, and from 1993 all new cars on sale would require a catalytic converter as standard and so unleaded became the norm. By the dawn of the new century, these measures and diminished lead on other grades of petrol had slashed vehicle exhaust emissions by 90 per cent.

The average price of a gallon of petrol fluctuated throughout the 1980s, with the sharpest year-on-year hike being between the £1.28 of 1980 and £1.60 of 1981 – in the teeth of a particularly aggressive recession. It would then peak at £1.99 in 1985 before drifting back down to £1.70 in 1987 and creeping back up to £1.85 in 1989. Our addiction to cars and driving was ruthlessly exploited by the Treasury. In 1980, tax accounted for 45.2 per cent of a gallon's cost at the pump, and that steadily rose to 63.9 per cent by 1989.

One of the most radical changes in everyday motoring was *where* we actually filled up our tanks.

In 1980, there were 25,527 outlets selling petrol in the UK, but by 1990 that had shrunk to 19,465, with on average 2.8 per cent fewer every year. Compare that with the peak number, in 1967, of 39,958.

Much of the change is accounted for by spacious, purpose-built 'filling stations', constructed by the fuel companies themselves, and the dwindling number of garages or workshops with a few pumps at the front. At the new sites, with their brightly lit shops selling snacks, cigarettes, newspapers and other 'impulse buys', self-service was almost universal, with a forecourt attendant now a rarity.

Another relatively new fixture was a customer-friendly diesel pump. Until sales of diesel-engined Volkswagens and Peugeots gathered momentum at the tail end of the 1970s, diesel was usually dispensed at a standalone pump marked DERV for Diesel-Engined Road Vehicle) in an oily black, where there was space for lorries and other commercial vehicles. Now, and especially after Vauxhall and Ford added diesel models, the pump joined the others under the canopy and was marked 'Diesel'.

Supermarket chain Tesco had sold its first petrol in 1974, and by the 1980s its major rivals were opening forecourts all over the country – yet another nail in the coffin of the village garage and the small, independent petrol station. Nevertheless, new chains kept springing up to challenge them and also the major brands like BP, Shell, Texaco and Esso. Heron was one, developing a chain of 200 sites selling its own 'Big H' juice from 1986.

This concentration of sales among a few large companies was mirrored in car accessory shops, where chains, Halfords in particular, could offer cheaper prices, wider ranges and self-service, which made local high street shops uncompetitive. The company opened its first out-of-town superstore in Croydon in 1984, and many more would follow.

Kwik Fit was another national giant, this time selling and fitting replacement tyres, batteries and exhausts. It was one of Britain's very first retailers to link sales to stock via computers, which were installed at all its branches in 1981 and meant popular lines were re-ordered from suppliers automatically.

Cars now had most things you might require as standard equipment, but for niceties like this in-car vacuum cleaner – it could be powered using car battery terminals – motor accessory shops, such as Halfords, were still the place to go.

It then spent £10 million on its annoyingly catchy TV ad campaign entitled 'You can't get better than a Kwik Fit Fitter', which ran from 1984 to 1989. As a result, Kwik Fit became a household name, and swallowed up rivals like Chessington Tyres and Charlie Browns, although the rising number of cars overall meant there were still plenty of sales to be had for small local outfits. ATS, the

Both the AA and the RAC introduced brand new computer systems during this decade in their attempts to reach stranded motorists over more rapidly.

former Associated Tyre Services, became the other big national chain, and started offering its mobile services to company car fleets.

Throughout the 1980s, the MoT test remained largely unchanged. In 1978, it had gained several important new inspection points that covered windscreen washers, wipers, indicators, spotlights and the horn, and also established minimum standards for structural rust and the exhaust system. Then, in 1991 petrol emissions, anti-lock brakes and rear seatbelts all joined the checklist. The only real 1980s change affected taxis and the few cars with eight seats, which now needed to be tested after one year in use, not the usual three.

AA membership passed the 7 million mark in 1987. The rescue organisation launched its Home Start service in 1982, and upped its game in 1986 with the introduction of its 'Command & Control' computerised communication system to replace all previous paper-based workings. The smaller RAC started its rival 'Advanced Computer Aided Rescue System' the following year, and there was growing competition from Green Flag, a national network of garages-on-call with real local knowledge for a super-swift response via its National Breakdown and Recovery Club. It began in Bradford in 1971 and offered twenty-four-hour recovery by rerouting its phone system to mechanics' homes at night!

Having a poorly car was one thing; having it wilfully damaged, or even removed altogether, was another. 'Car crime' was a depressing 1980s phenomenon, and a cause of huge concern.

Although car theft had been a problem since the start of mass motoring in Britain in the early 1920s, it was relatively insignificant, and only increased proportionately to the number of vehicles on the road. Between 1980 and 1990 the number of stolen cars annually rose from 324,354 to 494,000.

Theft *from* vehicles, though, jumped alarmingly, from 294,948 notified offences in 1980 to a massive 772,900 in 1990. In fact, in that year, car crime of all sorts increased by a whopping 24 per cent over 1989, representing 28 per cent of all recorded crime. The 'risk per car' was getting out of control and organised thieves chasing a profit, rather than joyriders, seemed to be having a field day; in 1970, 89 per cent of stolen vehicles were recovered but by 1990 this had slumped to just 66 per cent. Likewise, in 1980, London's Metropolitan Police recorded 63,906 incidents of 'unauthorised taking' – as opposed to outright theft – but by 1990 this had fallen 39 per cent to 38,943.

There were already two parliamentary working groups examining car security and car crime when, in 1986, Prime Minister Margaret Thatcher fostered links between the car industry and the British Standards Institution and they worked together on better mechanical locking systems, at the same time as raising awareness among drivers to increase prevention.

The work led to vastly better security measures for car radios and hi-fis, window-etched glass, centralised power locking, deadlocks, vehicle alarms and, eventually, immobilisers. All these made the 1990s a rather more reassuring era for our cars.

Austin Maestro/Montego, 1983

The Maestro is often lampooned as one of Britain's worst-ever cars, yet that's a misinformed verdict. It was far from being terrible.

Okay, its oddly chiselled contours and scalloped sides rob it of much elegance, but here was a roomy and practical family chariot, sized mid-way between the Ford Escort and Ford Sierra. Thanks to well-sorted, all-round coil-spring suspension, road manners were good, and there was a wide choice of engine and trim options.

The car, under its LC10 codename, was championed by Sir Michael Edwardes as he struggled between 1977 and 1982 to haul BL back to viability. It was conceived as a straightforward, conventional front-wheel drive model, avoiding the costly and weird rubber and gas suspensions used in the Mini, Metro, Maxi and Allegro.

Its engines let it down. The very basic 1.3-litre owed its roots to pre-Second World War models, while the larger one – as found in the MG model – was BL's new 1.6-litre R Series, and that came with carburettor problems; it was swiftly replaced by the S Series, a hasty update. The Maestro's key gimmick

WHAT THEY SAID AT THE TIME

'Although it's not flawless, this unpretentious workhorse version of the new Maestro delivers a combination of performance, accommodation and all-round economy that rivals will find hard to equal. Weaknesses include a lack of a five-speed option and mediocre mechanical refinement.'

Motor magazine in April 1983 on the £4,955 Maestro 1.3L.

The Maestro was no looker, admittedly, but the car has an undeservedly poor reputation, and it was, after all, the tenth best-selling car of the whole decade.

A fleet of Montego estates serve as courtesy cars at the 1989 Wimbledon tennis championships.

was its all-digital dashboard, with LED warning lights, trip computer and synthesised audio alerts voiced by actress Nicolette McKenzie.

The Austin Montego followed in 1984, a saloon version of the Maestro with different styling front and back. There were sporty MG editions of both, and later on turbo diesels too. The trouble was, by the mid-1980s, car industry benchmarks were hurtling upwards. The Maestro/Montego was competent, but nowhere near its Japanese competitors, or Volkswagen's MkII Golf, for build quality.

WHO LOVED IT?

If you had a 'Buy British' mentality then it had to be a Maestro or a Montego as a roomy, mid-range family car; most owners were satisfied with the broadly good service to be had from both. Many others found there were better alternatives that didn't have the British duo's drawbacks.

This is the 1.6LX edition of the Montego, basically the same car as the Maestro only with a conventional saloon back end.

BMW 3 Series MkII, 1983

BMW's original 3 Series was the compact sports saloon that opened the door for lots more buyers to become marque disciples, despite being quite expensive and a long way from enjoying its favoured company car status of today.

Anxious to build steadily on its success, BMW played extremely safe with the MkII, codenamed E30, updating and refining the successful concept but keeping the essence the same. Hence there was a bulging menu of four- and straight-six-cylinder engines beginning at 1.6-litre and culminating in the powerful 2.5 325i with 171bhp of growling power going to its back wheels. For those living in snowy parts of Europe and North America, there was also the 325iX, with four-wheel drive (BMW's first car so-equipped), although only a handful of these came to the UK, in left-hand drive form only.

The 2.0-litre 320i was the big seller and, like other versions, it could be had as a two- or four-door saloon, a four-door Touring estate and an ultra-smart two-door convertible, with an optional power-operated hood. The M3, meanwhile, was a racing car tamed for road use, with up to 215bhp on tap, close-ratio gearbox, limited slip differential and flared wings embracing fat alloy wheels.

The rear suspension on this new model had been thoroughly worked over, to avoid the tail-happy hairiness of the previous 323i.

From a design viewpoint, the E30 developed the aura of discreet good taste of the old 3 Series and larger 5 Series models. With superb driving dynamics and exquisite build quality, they were in demand from the off.

WHO LOVED IT?

The ebullient 1980s was in full swing when this excellent new car arrived, just in time to ride the wave of optimism and soaring ambitions of Brits making their way in Margaret Thatcher's Britain. As a consequence, sales soared and BMW prospered like never before; a massive 2.2 million were sold in all.

The discreetly handsome lines of the four-door 3 Series were soon familiar around the more affluent parts of Britain.

Particularly pleasing are the lines of the 3 Series convertible because the hood folded away and was concealed below a neat metal cover.

This Touring edition of the 3 Series arrived in 1988 to become the first estate car BMW had ever offered.

WHAT THEY SAID AT THE TIME

'The rough edges of BMW's quickest small saloon have been honed to produce a refined sporting thoroughbred which is hard to fault. Handling is safer but just as much fun, which, along with the good driving position, powerful brakes and excellent transmission, make it a fine driver's car.'

Motor magazine in February 1983 on the £9,655 323i.

Fiat Uno, 1983

For so long the master of the appealing small car, Fiat pulled off yet another masterstroke with the Uno to replace the 127. It proved astonishingly popular: at the time of writing, at the end of 2013, the 1983-vintage model is *still* being churned out in Brazil as a low-cost economy car (albeit one now glaringly lagging behind modern cars for safety), with production inching past 8.8 million. That makes it the fourth bestselling single car design of all time.

The Uno was designed by Giorgetto Giugiaro, who had been experimenting with more upright car shapes since the late 1970s. It was taller than similar superminis like the Fiesta and Metro, with an airy cabin and commanding seating positions in both the three- and five-door models. It started a trend for such shapes that reversed years of cars getting lower and sleeker but, ultimately, less comfortable to access and exit. Its shape made it spacious but also, by virtue of the abruptly truncated rear end, surprisingly aerodynamic. This in turn helped towards lively performance and very good fuel economy.

The 127's 0.9-litre overhead-valve and 1.1/1.3 overhead-camshaft engines were carried over, but in 1985 Fiat's all-new 1.0-litre FIRE engine replaced the smallest unit. It was lighter, simpler, more responsive and easier on petrol. There would also be a 1.3 Turbo with 105bhp for boy

WHAT THEY SAID AT THE TIME

'It's a forgiving little car which gives plenty of "seat-of-the-pants" feel and inspires confidence under all-round conditions. Its performance and accommodation can't be bettered by any of its rivals.'

Motor magazine in June 1983 on the £3,690 Uno 55 Comfort (1.1).

Reversing years during which family cars had become lower and ever less easy to access, the Uno's styling stood tall and airy.

racers, with an incredible 130mph top speed, and a 1.7-litre diesel.

All Unos handled superbly thanks to brilliant independent suspension, MacPherson struts upfront and a twist-beam rear axle located with telescopic dampers and coil springs.

Inside, early Unos featured control pods instead of stalks, for fingertip-actuated functions with both hands remaining gripped on the wheel. More no-brainer ease was added on the Selecta model in 1987 with a continuously variable automatic transmission.

The five-door Uno was the most practical, and the 1.7-litre diesel from 1987 onwards made it very frugal.

WHO LOVED IT?

The Uno was popular in Britain. The 1983–89 MkI shifted an impressive 190,000 examples, making it one of the leaders in its market area. The well-deserved accolade of 1984 European Car of the Year helped but, really, there was little to dislike and much to enjoy.

Land Rover 110/90, 1983

In the peaks and troughs of fortune inflicted on the post-war British motor industry, the trusty four-wheel drive Land Rover remained consistently successful, loved by farmers at home and abroad and everyone else from coastguards to councils. Changes were few, so well suited was the basic design to the toughest off-road duties.

But once Land Rover Ltd was formed and the marque gained its independence in 1978, things changed. Company bosses first gave the long-wheelbase Land Rover more power with a V8 engine option, but that failed to address its lamentable, bone-shaking on-road comfort. With new 4x4 rivals arriving from Japan – high-riding, four-wheel drive off-roaders in comfortable estate car form, but far cheaper than a Range Rover – the pressure was on.

A more civilised Land Rover eventually appeared as the 110 and 90 (both indicating their extended wheelbase length in inches) in 1983 and '84 respectively. The main news was the all-round coil-spring suspension on a Range Rover-style chassis, ousting the masochistic old leaf spring set-up. Petrol or diesel four-cylinder engines now thankfully came with a five-speed manual

WHAT THEY SAID AT THE TIME

'The V8 90 must now rival the Range Rover as the best off-road car in the world. The shorter wheelbase and steeper angles of approach and departure mean even better agility over tortuous terrain'

Autocar magazine in June 1981 on the £2,860 Panda 45.

Land Rovers had always been invaluable to the emergency services, and so it continued; this is a police patrol 110 Station Wagon.

This ghosted image of the 110 shows its inner workings, with the new coil-spring suspension clear to see.

WHO LOVED IT?

These changes to traditional Land Rovers addressed their major flaws but left their indomitable off-road capability intact and, for the toughest work, unmatched. People wanting an industrial-strength four-wheel drive stayed faithful, even though the 110 and 90 were a little too raw to be considered 'lifestyle' 4x4s.

gearbox for reasonably tolerable motorway driving.

A wider track boosted stability and was obvious through new flared wheel arches in body-matching polyurethane plastic. A Series III V8-style nose was now standard, fronted by a new plastic grille, because a V8 engine (with four-speed manual gearbox) was offered in short- and long-wheelbase Landies. In 1985 the V8 model was gifted a five-speed gearbox too, four-cylinder capacities were increased to 2.5-litre, and all models saw their crude sliding windows replaced with wind-down items.

These Land Rovers, largely unchanged, are still being made today as the Defender series.

A Land Rover 90 as a pick-up in its natural habitat – the English countryside.

Mercedes-Benz 190, 1983

Mercedes-Benz in Stuttgart had had to look on aghast as its upstart rival BMW in Munich pulled in tens of thousands of new prestige car customers, attracted to the 3 Series. Throughout the early 1980s they were hard at work on their own interpretation of a relatively affordable and compact saloon, under the project code W201, and the wraps were off in December 1982.

It was a brand new design, smaller than the 200 Series but utterly redolent of both that and the large S Class; the classic proportions were entirely Merc in their appearance yet there was a subtle wedge profile that hinted at the considerable aerodynamic fettling that had taken place.

Although clearly in the traditional Mercedes saloon idiom, the 190 was subtly wedge-shaped.

WHAT THEY SAID AT THE TIME

'The 190E is the best riding car Mercedes has ever made, and it combines this with taut, safe handling. Overall standards of refinement are very good, too, though BMW's six-cylinder-engined 3 Series cars are mechanically sweeter.'

Motor magazine in September 1984 on the £10,640 190E.

Believe it or not, this was the most compact car Mercedes had ever offered, as it battled with arch-rival the BMW 3 Series.

WHO LOVED IT?

This was exactly the right car for the time and sales of the 190 Series were brisk from the start, in Britain as elsewhere. It was always relatively pricey but the build quality was fantastic, and the range developed over the years to offer newer, more powerful engines. By the finish of manufacture in 1993, almost 1.9 million had been sold, of which over 450,000 were 190Ds.

The sober dashboard layout greeting the driver nevertheless offered excellent clarity; note the storage slots for six cassette tapes above the radio!

The seats in a 190 were very comfortable and supportive, but the standard car offered few gizmos – a radio and electric windows came at an extra cost.

As the 190, it came with a carburettor 2.0-litre engine, and as the 190E there was Bosch electronic fuel injection. The 190D had a notably quiet 2.0 diesel. It was a very stable and fine-handling car to drive, due in major part to a patented five-link independent rear suspension system and lightweight rear axle. Clearly, this excellent chassis could handle more power, and two years after launch came the be-spoilered 190E 2.3-16, with a 16-valve cylinder head design courtesy of British race engine specialist Cosworth. It turned out to be quite a formidable saloon car racer, including in the hands of a young Ayrton Senna.

Mercedes claimed the high-strength sheet steel it used made the 190 light, but it also admitted that it was over-engineered, and diligent attention to safety and strength resulted in cramped space for rear seat passengers. Still, they did endow the 190 with a conventional handbrake between the two front seats, to free up space in the front footwells where Mercs traditionally featured a foot-operated version.

Mitsubishi Shogun, 1983

The sport-utility vehicle, or SUV, finally matured into a truly consumer-friendly product thanks to Mitsubishi's four-wheel drive Shogun (that name was only for the UK, mind; it was the Montero in Spanish-speaking territories and the USA, and the Pajero elsewhere). Instantly and widely imitated by catch-up competitors, it was a ground-up design, with no throwbacks to previous vehicles and no carry-over components to somehow render the driving experience a tank- or truck-like one.

Presenting the 'two-box' shape of a typical supermini but to a far larger scale, the earliest Shogun came as a neat three-door estate

WHAT THEY SAID AT THE TIME

'Comfortable driving position and light, car-like controls make the Shogun easy to drive; an ideal recreational vehicle. The Shogun is a good all-terrain vehicle, but it's pricey and luggage access is restricted'

Autocar magazine in April 1984 on the £10,500 Shogun Turbo Diesel.

which, while still a large car, was not threateningly so. An imposing five-door model soon joined it. The bonnet line was low and the cabin tall, making entry and exit through generously wide doors far easier than the 'mounting' needed on, for example, truck-based SUVs from the US. A thoughtfully designed interior made the most of the copious quantities of light streaming in through the big windows.

The original Pajero/Shogun came as a three-door estate with generous glazing, and a remarkably large pair of wing mirrors!

The front torsion bar suspension allied to traditional leaf springs at the back conspired for a decent on-tarmac ride, astonishingly car-like. The four-wheel drive system was selectable, with the rear wheels

Anyone without the wheelbarrow-full of requisite readies to afford a Range Rover could get almost everything they wanted in a Shogun, and thousands did. British sales were as strong in the deep countryside as they were in the suburbs, and it massively increased the demand for SUVs.

Five doors, a raised roof and an extended wheelbase made the Shogun look huge, but it was actually quite wieldy to handle on-road.

only driven for everyday use. The Shogun was the first ever turbo diesel passenger car to emerge from Japan, and this was an excellent performer. There were four-cylinder and thirsty V6 petrol options too.

Even Mitsubishi was amazed when a near-standard Shogun scored a legendary victory in the production car class of the Paris–Dakar desert race in 1982 on its maiden attempt. Customers loved it, and the Shogun's

runaway success made Land Rover resolve to match it, which it belatedly did with the Discovery of 1989.

Nissan Micra, 1983

This little 1.0-litre supermini took its bow in 1982 in Japan as the Nissan Match. It arrived in the UK in that hazy crossover period when the company was ditching its old Datsun brand name for the Nissan one. That's why early Micras bear tiny 'Datsun' nameplates on their tailgates.

There is unsubstantiated web gossip that the design was by Italy's Giugiaro, because the Micra's stance, unusually tall and upright for the day, was similar to design themes the company was espousing, which were evident in its styling for the Fiat Uno. More likely the Micra was rushed out to combat the small-and-tall Honda City, a runaway hit in Japan in 1981. One thing's for sure, though: the Micra was plain when new, and it's positively nondescript today.

The forgettable image, however, masked an uncommonly refined drivetrain. The 988cc single-cam engine was all-aluminium and very smooth, and its lightness upfront lent the non-power steering a remarkable ease, something mirrored by the brakes (front discs only) and clutch. There was a late-life hike in engine size in 1989 to 1.2 litres, raising power output from a mild 50bhp to a very slightly more athletic 60bhp.

Plasticky blandness prevailed inside too, although it was roomy and well equipped. The car's truly impressive aspect was its remarkable build quality and durability. True, its ranks of elderly owners were hardly likely to abuse their Micras, but these cars lasted and lasted. In 2007, some

WHAT THEY SAID AT THE TIME

'It is not as keenly priced as other Datsun/Nissan models, but with its excellent blend of performance and economy, capable handling and slick five-speed transmission, it represents a very competitive package.'

Motor magazine in July 1983 on the £4,150 Micra GL.

The Micra was never going to set the world on fire with either looks or performance, but reliability was its strong suit.

thirteen years after manufacture of this original Micra ceased, 28 per cent of all the cars sold in the UK were still going strong, compared to 1.6 per cent of Metros, 3.3 per cent of Ford Fiesta MkI/IIs, and 2.7 per cent of Fiat Unos.

WHO LOVED IT?

The Micra was intended as nothing more than a trusty runabout, and Britain's less excitable drivers, especially older and shrewder ones, bought it in droves. It was a key breakthrough car for Japan in the UK, more so even than the Toyota Corolla. By 1987, it was the UK's top choice for driving schools, such was its forgiving nature.

A neat little effort, the Micra, and one that was so easy to drive that it soon became Britain's top driving school car.

Peugeot 205, 1983

Throughout its fifteen years in Peugeot showrooms, over 5 million 205s were sold, but the acclaim it garnered made it a legend in its own lifetime, while the GTi models were some of the most thrilling, best-loved sporting cars of the 1980s. *Autocar* magazine stated in 1991 it was 'still the best small car' – and that for a lowly 1.1 model tested against Ford's then all-new Fiesta MkIII. *Car* magazine has declared it the single best car the 1980s produced, bar none.

The neat and timeless Pininfarina styling was certainly a factor in its appeal; throughout its time on sale, it was never once facelifted. But it was the overall right-ness of the 205 that shone through – the superbly roomy cabin thanks to compact torsion bar suspension, the supple ride, the lightness that meant even the smallest engine felt punchy. Perhaps

WHAT THEY SAID AT THE TIME

'Grippy and responsive chassis sets new standards of handling and road-holding. Fast and fun, the 205 GTi lives up to its promise of affordable excitement, and runs circles around similarly priced hotshots.'

Motor magazine in May 1984 on the £6,295 205 GTi.

Fun, fun, fun: the 205 GTi, here in 1.9-litre form, instantly became *the* hot hatchback of the 1980s, with power and torque in abundance.

For a small, affordable car, the 205 offered legendary robustness; this faithful example had covered 338,000 miles when this picture was taken.

most of all, it was the high-torque XUD7 diesel engine available in the car, a motor so quiet and powerful it single-handedly turned sentiment in favour of small diesels.

The 205 GTi, with its lowered suspension and widened wheel arches, grabbed the hot hatchback baton from Volkswagen and sprinted away with it. The initial 1.6-litre edition with 115bhp on tap had enthusiasts foaming at the mouth. Here was a true successor to the Mini Cooper, a yardstick for driver satisfaction, acceleration and handling. Bit of a hard ride, though. And then in 1986 the 1.9-litre car added an extra 15bhp and lots of torque for overtaking, taking the GTi to thrilling new levels. Its legacy lingers because modern hot hatchbacks are still sometimes measured against it for that elusive 'fun factor'.

WHO LOVED IT?

All classes, ages and sexes of driver loved the 205 in its various incarnations, and it was a constant bestseller. In 1991, for instance, the by then 8-year-old 205 still accounted for 3 per cent of the whole UK market. Interestingly, Peugeot's reputation for quality in those days is borne out by the fact that you do still see quite a few 205s continuing to give reliable service even today.

Vauxhall Nova, 1983

General Motors was able to begin with a totally clean sheet of paper for what became the Nova. Despite the popularity of the outgoing Vauxhall Chevette/Opel Kadett, this would be the first time the company had created a truly credible supermini rival to the Ford Fiesta, Austin Metro and Volkswagen Polo. And it was one of three highly capable new entries into the sector in 1983, alongside the Peugeot 205 and Fiat Uno. Plus, it was built in a brand new plant in wholly new territory for GM – Spain.

First seen in September 1982 as the Opel Corsa, the name was changed for Britain to Vauxhall Nova for its launch in spring 1983. The long delay was due in part to union protests that the car wasn't being made in the UK.

The classic supermini package of front transverse engine, front-wheel drive and spacious three-door hatchback was adopted; the smallest engine was a pushrod carryover from the now-obsolete Opel Kadett City, although the rest of the engine range, with overhead camshafts, was brand new.

The three-door car had distinctive and sporty blistered wheel arches,

WHAT THEY SAID AT THE TIME

'GM's long-awaited supermini sets no new standards in the small car class but it does impress with its all-round competence. Worthy of note are the potentially excellent fuel economy, handling and brakes. Competitively priced.'

Motor magazine in May 1983 on the £3,636 Nova 1.0.

The Nova did nothing exceptionally but everything reasonably well, and that was enough to ensure strong 1980s sales.

although the subsequent five-door did with plain wings and was pretty bland-looking, and the range departed from the European norm with the addition of two- and four-door saloons.

The Spanish-built Nova was available in saloon form, with either two or four doors, and also as a five-door hatchback – no other supermini offered so many permutations.

The Nova was not especially sparkling in the driving pleasure department, especially beside the class-leading 205 and Uno. Still, this was no bar to its popularity and, indeed, its longevity; it was reliable to own, cheap to run, and very practical. A diesel engine, supplied by Japan's Isuzu, expanded the range choice in 1987, alongside a rapid, good-looking GSi model with a 1.6-litre engine and 100bhp on tap.

WHO LOVED IT?

GM made over 3 million of these cars, with nearly a sixth of them sold as Vauxhalls, rendering the Nova one of the marque's top sellers and a common sight across the country. Second-hand, and especially with the 1.0-litre motor, it was a favourite as a first car, particularly when parents had a say in the matter.

Volkswagon Golf MkII, 1983

Here is one of the truly great cars of the 1980s. Volkswagen's second-generation Golf was everything its illustrious, trend-setting predecessor had been, and so much more.

Not wanting to tamper with a winning formula, VW took the original Giugiaro lines and worked them over to make the car bigger and roomier. It was about 7in longer and 2in wider, with a longer wheelbase and a wider footprint. A much more comfortable interior was another part of the £500 million update project.

Of course, the car's weight grew from 840kg to 920kg but, apart from the weedy 1.1-litre model that was soon axed anyway, it didn't feel any more torpid because it was hugely

WHAT THEY SAID AT THE TIME

'It has a beautifully smooth, responsive engine which is mated to a satisfyingly closely-spaced set of gear ratios; it offers incredibly reassuring amounts of grip and traction; and it possesses arrow-like straight stability through the speed range.'

Autocar magazine in May 1984 on the £7,867 Golf GTi.

Volkswagen was spot on with its second-generation Golf, setting benchmarks of comfort and quality that few rivals could equal.

more aerodynamic. The 1.3 and 1.6 engines were later joined by a 1.8, while the 1.6 diesel was given the option of a turbocharger to make it more powerful and lively. The Golf everyone wanted, though, was the GTi, which returned in 1.8-litre, 112bhp form and retained the old car's scintillating delivery of driving thrills. This included a 119mph top speed and 0–60mph in 8.5 seconds, with all-round disc brakes. A 16-valve engine head option in 1986 made the car even faster, although many purists preferred the original.

Where other cars felt flimsy or cheap, the Golf was strong and rigorously engineered, and just about any model was confidence-inspiring to drive. Within a few years, the car also brought standard catalytic converters, anti-lock brakes and four-wheel drive to the family hatchback category. In 1987, one of its few faults, for British drivers, was fixed, when windscreen wipers correctly positioned for right-hand drive cars were fitted, but another feature that many liked – the fixed front quarterlight – was dropped.

These renderings show how VW retained the character of the original Golf while making the new car bigger all-round.

WHO LOVED IT?

Although always a little more costly than direct rivals, the MkII proved immensely popular in the UK from its introduction in March 1984 right up until it was replaced in 1992. The car was current when the total Golf production tally reached 10 million in 1988. The one-millionth Golf GTi, a MkII, was delivered in November 1990.

Fast, delightful to drive, and cool to be seen in, the MkII Golf GTi had it all, and could be had with 8- or 16-valve engines.

MK II Golf

1980s Dream Cars

The 1970s had only just faded out when Audi turned the supercar world on its head. It was March 1980 and its new arrival at the Geneva Motor Show managed to hog most of the limelight without a wedge-shaped profile, a stupidly enormous engine, a racing car layout or even doors that opened in a bizarre fashion. Pedants at the German company insisted everyone use a lower case 'q' when referring to the Quattro but, despite that, it was quite the capital car.

The boxy-looking four-seater coupé appeared mundane enough externally, but its cocktail of permanent four-wheel drive allied to a turbocharged five-cylinder engine was a brand new mix. A performance 4x4 as a conventional road car had appeared in the 1960s as the Jensen FF, but in the intervening period vehicles with all wheels driven had been almost wholly utilitarian affairs. The Quattro's tarmac-gripping road-holding was little short of

The Audi Quattro rewrote the supercar rulebook in 1980 by combining four-wheel drive with a turbocharged engine, and later added anti-lock brakes to boost driving safety.

Although a hugely desirable and very exciting car, the mid-engined M1 was a short-lived venture for BMW, putting a mere 450 examples in the hands of wealthy customers, only a tiny number of them in Britain.

sensational, and 60mph from standstill could be attained in 6.5 seconds, although the engine's turbo boost could cut in quite savagely. Within a year a further novel attribute, anti-lock brakes, vastly enhanced overall drivability. It came initially in left-hand drive only, and cost £14,500, but if you wanted the most technologically advanced performance road car on earth then this was it.

The Quattro stood in stark contrast to the other noteworthy German supercar of 1980, the mid-engined BMW M1. The chassis had been fine-tuned by Lamborghini, which was all set to build it too, but the scheme went awry and BMW spent a fortune on a complicated production run of just 450 cars. It was amazing to drive, with the company's 3.5-litre straight-six amidships, yet only a handful of private imports ever reached the UK.

The other premium German marques brought their own 'ultimate' cars to the party in the early '80s. Porsche, for example, was already acclaimed both for the long-running 911 and the newer, front-engined 928, but added a new facet to its catalogue in 1982 with the very first Cabriolet edition of the 911 – previously,

It took until 1982 for Porsche to take the plunge and offer a completely open-topped version of its classic 911, the Cabriolet.

all open versions of the rear-engined classic had had a fixed roll-over bar and 'Targa' lift-out roof panel. A Porsche 911 was the car that 'young, upwardly-mobile professionals', the famously annoying 'Yuppies' of the 1980s, all aspired to. Or so those who couldn't afford one claimed!

And then there was Mercedes-Benz, which in 1981 introduced the suave and stylish SEC coupé edition of its masterful new S Class. All the side windows could be rolled down for a sleek pillar-less look, and the V8 engine range eventually spanned 3.8 to 5.6 litres, all with four-speed automatic gearboxes. It offered effortless, albeit expensive, elegance.

In Italy, authentic supercar land, Ferrari struck out with something novel in 1980: a four-seater mid-engined car. The Mondial 8 might have appeared a touch ungainly beside the two-seater 308 models, but it was a whole lot more practical, and what's more the performance was damn near as good.

But while the family man could now continue to enjoy Ferrari driving, the hedonist could also indulge him- or herself with the 288 GTO of 1984. Less than 300 of these 308-based specials were made to qualify the twin-turbo coupé, with its 400bhp of power and 366lb ft of torque, for Group B rallying, but after that class was cancelled almost all GTOs were road cars ... and capable of 190mph.

Imposing, impressive and very expensive, the SEC was the coupé version of the S-Class, making it probably the most desirable contemporary Mercedes-Benz of all.

Above: The hunkered-down, purposeful face of the Ferrari 288 GTO, a twin-turbo supercar that was capable of 190mph.

Left: This four-seater mid-engined Ferrari was the Mondial 8, introduced in 1980 and hugely increasing the marque's appeal to devotees who found themselves in the family way.

That sort of speed rather overshadowed the 180mph you might be able to coax out of your new Lamborghini Countach LP500, with a V12 engine enlarged to 5.0 litres from the previous 4.0 but still offering little extra power until the 46-valve cylinder head engine arrived in 1985. Yet for flamboyant image, there was little to touch it, even if its optional massive rear spoiler was mostly ineffective apart from drawing attention to the car itself. Tiny numbers of Countachs were built throughout the 1980s.

Meanwhile, the DeLorean DMC-12 had barely begun to impress American buyers with its gullwing doors

Broad church: Lamborghini's Countach continued throughout the 1980s as one of the most dramatic cars on the road, although its rear spoiler was more for show than go.

and brushed stainless steel body panels when the enterprise, based in Northern Ireland and bankrolled by the British government, collapsed in bankruptcy. You heard an awful lot about the car on news bulletins, and no doubt loved seeing it in the *Back to the Future* movies of the 1980s, but it never got the chance to go on sale in its country of origin.

The Alpine A610 GTA used the same Renault V6 engine as the DeLorean, similarly mounted at the back, and

a few of these fantastic, French-built sports cars did come to the UK from 1986 onwards. In 2.5-litre Turbo form, it was shatteringly fast, with 165mph attainable and a 0–60mph time of just 5.7 seconds, and road manners clearly related to Alpine's racing cars of the past.

Yet Britain had its own offbeat car companies, like Lotus and TVR. For the former, this was the decade of the Esprit, which received a turbocharger itself in 1980 and in 1988 was subject to a total restyle that, by common consent, gave this mid-engined junior supercar an excellent new lease of life. TVR took the opposite tack, going for a front engine without a turbo in its all-new Tasmin of 1980. After a shaky launch straight into an economic slump, the car's bacon was saved when a Rover V8 engine was installed; the resulting 350i put the Blackpool firm on the map at

The dramatic gullwing doors of the DeLorean DMC-12 weren't enough to save the company from oblivion … but they looked pretty cool in the *Back to the Future* movies with Michael J. Fox.

Renault V6 power in the tail of the 1986 Alpine GTA gave this unusual French GT sensational performance.

In the 1980s, Jaguar took its XJS racing, and it put up some magnificent showings in the European Touring Car Championship, giving the newly floated Coventry company a big image boost.

last, and would lead to a bewildering array of spin-off models all with one common factor: massive power.

The 1980s was quite a good period for Jaguar. It started with the automatic XJS being declared, at 151mph and with the 0–60mph sprint taking just 6.6 seconds, the world's fastest automatic car. The XJS took Jaguar racing again in 1982, competing in the European Touring Car Championship where it won its first victory for nineteen years at the Tourist Trophy event. The company was privatised with a wildly successful Stock Market flotation in 1984, and in 1988 it revealed its stunning XJ220 mid-engined supercar, which would belatedly come to life in the 1990s.

By comparison, Aston Martin had an altogether tougher time. Although first deliveries of its sensational Lagonda began in 1980, at the same time as its Bulldog concept car was unveiled, the company faced an almighty struggle to fund both the V8 Vantage Zagato of 1985 and the all-new Virage launched in 1988. Along the way, its Tickford division also created the 140mph Tickford Capri – something of a junior Aston Vantage itself. But it got there in the end, thanks to a takeover by Ford, and the venerable marque lived to see another day.

A sporting mojo was revived by Bentley with its Mulsanne Turbo of 1982 and carried on valiantly by the 1985 Turbo R, both just a tiny bit thirsty but with a thunderous performance ... and top speed limited to 135mph as there were simply no available tyres that could handle more from the 2.8-ton behemoth!

Never officially sold in the UK was the fourth-generation Chevrolet Corvette of 1983, although a few examples of America's only real sports car did end up on British roads, and Lotus created a special engine for

Britain's Aston Martin was in a constant struggle for survival during almost the whole of the 1980s, but this didn't stop it launching some exciting new cars, such as this V8 Vantage with Zagato bodywork.

After years in the doldrums as a half-hearted companion marque
to Rolls-Royce, Bentley made a sudden return to greatness
with this turbocharged edition of the Mulsanne saloon in 1982,
identified externally by its painted radiator shell.

the ultimate incarnation, the 180mph ZR-1. Another vehicle hotly debated but almost never seen here was the outrageous Lamborghini LM002, a hulking great V12-engined off-road machine which one magazine memorably christened the 'Rambo Lambo'.

Hugely costly revivals included one from old-established coachbuilder Hooper, whose Empress II was a controversial rebody of a Bentley Turbo R for a crazy £270,000, and the Jensen Interceptor, which was raised from the grave in 1988 as a living antique with a £100,000 price tag.

But the two ultimate driving machines that did arrive in the late 1980s were very much from the supercar establishment.

If you had £270,000 spare in 1987 then you could have spent it on one of these, a Hooper Empress II, a hand-crafted luxury car based on a Bentley Turbo R. It was, at least, different.

The Ferrari F40, at 201mph, laid claim to be the fastest road car you could buy. It was stripped of everything that got in the way of visceral thrills in the lightweight composite-bodied two-seater, which meant carpet and door trim for a start, and was deafeningly noisy. Yet that was all part of the fun in celebrating the marque's 40th birthday by roaring from 0 to 60mph in 3.9 seconds.

The Porsche 959, meanwhile, went the other way, being easy to drive, with the twin-turbo flat-six engine featuring water-cooled cylinder heads, transmission a six-speed manual, and the ride height electronically adjustable. But, boy, could it move: 60mph was attained from rest in a mere 3.7 seconds, and one German motoring journalist managed to clock 197mph in one.

The Ferrari F40 of 1987 was created to celebrate Enzo Ferrari's fortieth year in the supercar business. It became the first production car in the world capable of hitting 200mph.

Ford Fiesta, 1984

Britain's favourite supermini had ruled the roost ever since it was launched in 1976. Popular as it still was, though, the Fiesta was well overdue an upgrade in the face of its many more modern imitators. But there was plenty of life in the old dog yet, so Ford chose to give the car a thorough working-over rather than replace it.

The whole front end was redesigned to be more modern and wind-cheating, and the tailgate continued the styling lines round from the sides. Changes to the dashboard meant there were almost entirely different designs for the lower and higher specification versions, which was pretty unusual for any model range.

The economy 1.0 and 1.1 engines, part of Ford's long-running Kent Series, were carried over virtually unchanged, with four-speed gearboxes. But there was a new 1.3, a CVH unit shared with the Escort, itself updated to a 1.4 lean-burn motor a couple of years later; the XR2i had a 1.6 CVH with a lusty 95bhp, and all the bigger-engined cars now came with a five-speed gearbox. A 1.6-litre diesel completed the parade.

WHAT THEY SAID AT THE TIME

'The Fiesta's age is not belied by its refinement – it has enough of that often elusive quality to remain competitive. Ford has done a good job of bringing the Fiesta into the 1980s with the facelift, and it has the further asset of above-average performance.'

Motor magazine in December 1984 on the £5,336 Fiesta 1300L.

If you wanted lively Fiesta motoring without the outright 'boy racer' image of the XR2, there was always this eager S model, with five-speed gearbox.

In its basic form, the fully revised Fiesta continued to offer trusty service and low running costs to a huge number of British drivers.

WHO LOVED IT?

The Fiesta was always near the top of the sales chart. Its excellent reputation for economy and value gave it universal appeal. This substantially revised version meant the Fiesta achieved its best-ever sales year in 1987, when Brits bought 150,000 of them. After 'Mustang' and 'Falcon', 'Fiesta' is Ford's longest-lived brand in continual production.

The same continuously variable automatic transmission as found in the Fiat Uno popped up in the revised Fiesta CTX model in 1987, allied to a 1.1-litre engine, so clearly tipped at the old lady market.

But there was only so far Ford could go with this Fiesta. Giving it the option of five doors, a choice many competitors now offered – even the Metro – was impossible and would have to wait until a totally new Fiesta took its bow in 1989.

Mitsubishi Space Wagon, 1984

There are a great many forgettable Mitsubishis that were on sale at one time or another during the 1980s. This, though, shouldn't be considered one of those also-rans because it was the first multi-purpose vehicle (MPV) or 'people-carrier' to go on UK sale. This was in 1984, a full year before the arrival of the Renault Espace.

Over the years, several car companies had tried to devise a car that could seat seven or eight in three rows of seats, but the result was often little more than a converted delivery van, and tended to be pretty ghastly to drive. Mitsubishi revealed a much more convincing, car-shaped and -sized concept design at the

WHAT THEY SAID AT THE TIME

'It is based on a saloon car floorpan but equipped with a taller body and, in this case, seating for six or seven. Performance is derived from a 1.8-litre engine. Economy is about class average.'

Autocar magazine in March 1985 on the £8,199 Space Wagon.

1979 Tokyo Motor Show. It was a tall and long estate car called the SSW, but it gained very little attention.

Yet three years later the car went on sale almost unchanged, and suddenly the world was alerted to the possibilities of an MPV.

They called it the Chariot in Japan, but for the UK when it arrived in 1984 it carried the name Space Wagon. We were offered two 1.8 engines, a petrol and, later, a turbo diesel. With 88bhp and 74bhp respectively, the front-wheel drive Space Wagon was certainly no ball of fire, especially with seven people on board with two upfront, three in the middle and two right at the back. But if you just happened to have five children – or even three and two grandparents to transport on regular days out – you were simply glad such a car now existed; particularly as it was like any other normal car to drive.

Seven proper seats were installed in the Space Wagon, using a standard saloon car floorpan so it was easy to drive.

Left: First of the many: little remembered today, the Mitsubishi Space Wagon was a true pioneer in MPVs.

WHO LOVED IT?

The Space Wagon was a godsend for large families, and it was much more comfortable for all occupants than long estate cars, such as Citroën's CX and Peugeot's 505, that simply squeezed two uncomfortable seats into the boot. Had a car like this come from a more mainstream manufacturer than Mitsubishi, UK sales would undoubtedly have been stronger.

Renault 5, 1984

Placing the engine across the car, transversely, instead of the in-line 'north–south' position of the hugely successful outgoing 5, was Renault's major achievement with its new supermini – or 'Supercinq' as they chose to title it.

This both brought it into line with all its crucial rivals and also produced a more roomy passenger compartment. A simpler MacPherson strut-based suspension system offered no downside in ride quality.

Engines were unchanged at the lower end of the range, with 1.4 models having five speeds, but were augmented by a 90bhp 1.7 for top-of-the-tree issues like the GTX and Baccara, this last being kitted out with leather upholstery, a standard sunroof and power steering. There was also a 1.6-litre diesel.

After the styling of recent Renaults had received lukewarm praise, the company turned to Marcello Gandini, the Italian designer of several Lamborghinis and Maseratis, for inspiration. He did an admirable job of modernising and tidying the

WHO LOVED IT?

Like its close rivals the Fiat Uno and Peugeot 205, the new 5 had the widest possible appeal across a spectrum starting with teenagers and ending with pensioners and taking in city commuter and boy racer in between. Even after the Clio usurped the car, a budget version of the 5 called the Campus sold very briskly in the UK for the first half of the 1990s, giving many a new driver their first set of wheels.

The Renault 5 GT Turbo was immensely fast for its size and price, forming a cut-price motor sport entry point for many.

Renault 5's well-liked profile. It became longer and wider, with its glazed area augmented by 20 per cent. A three-door came first, joined within months by a five-door.

There'd been sporty 5s in the past but the new 5 GT Turbo was very rapid and great fun. Its minimal weight of 850kg contributed to its electric acceleration – and wheelspin aplenty as the front alloys scrabbled for grip. Assuming the road was dry then its abundant torque pushed it to 60mph from rest in 7.5 seconds, quite something for its size and price.

The Supercinq did well throughout the 1980s, until the first of the Renault Clios arrived in 1990 to replace it.

Below: It's the 5 TSE model, showing off the extremely neat new styling of the spacious newcomer.

Above: The spiky-looking dashboard of the 'Supercinq' hasn't aged particularly well, but it looked cutting edge in 1984.

WHAT THEY SAID AT THE TIME

'Renault's new R5 has stepped on to the scene with some authority, offering thoroughly competitive performance, excellent handling, a superb ride and competitive pricing. Less good are the economy and the suppression of road noise.'

Motor magazine in February 1985 on the £4,400 5 TL.

Renault Espace, 1984

If all had gone to original plan, this should actually have been a Peugeot. Early designs for a spacious, seven-seater 'mini-van' with car-like driving characteristics – itself originally a US idea – were first brought to life in the Coventry styling studios of Chrysler Europe. In partnership with French specialist firm Matra, a prototype called the P16 was being readied when Peugeot acquired Chrysler's European outpost. But when the new

proprietors looked at the venture they decided it was simply too radical for European motorists, and promptly axed it.

Matra, anxious not to waste all its work, instead teamed up with Renault on a broadly similar car, and the two partners started work on the Espace in earnest in December 1982, with Matra getting ready to make the vehicle and Renault planning how they would market it.

The key tenets of the Espace were that it had to possess all the forgiving driving characteristics of a large, modern front-wheel drive car, and be uncommonly versatile inside. Hence the seven seats with the front two swivelling round to face the rear, where the central row of three seats could be folded and turned into a table, or else removed altogether for maximum cargo space. Today, many MPVs have these features; then, it

WHO LOVED IT?

Initial Espace sales in Britain were sluggish, as buyers nursed reservations about this seven-seater plastic box on wheels. Then, in 1985, orders rocketed, and production started at a second plant in 1987 to meet them. Buyers eagerly specified options like twin sunroofs, air-conditioning and four-wheel drive. In the end 182,000 examples of the original Espace were sold, several thousand of them to Brits.

WHAT THEY SAID AT THE TIME

'Hard to tell whether the so-called "people-carriers" are here to stay, but Renault has undoubtedly created the cleverest to date. Its massive 106cu ft of usable space is comprehensively adaptable for carrying either people or loads.'

Autocar magazine in September 1985 on the £11,555 Espace TXE.

Left: Definitely the car for people with hobbies and large families; the Espace concept was rejected by Peugeot, but rival Renault turned it into a winner.

Below: Supremely versatile seating meant the interior of the Espace could be configured however you wanted it.

was truly groundbreaking stuff to drivers of, say, a Cortina estate.

The partners reckoned the Espace would be a niche product, and so decided to manufacture the bodywork from low-investment glass fibre. This also gave it a low weight, endowing it with a nimbleness that belied its towering stance. Once you got used to the unnervingly raked windscreen that appeared to be several yards away from the steering wheel, you found the 2.0-litre petrol or turbo diesel engines made the Espace pretty pokey. Cornering, thanks to front-wheel drive, was also excellent.

Rover 200, 1984

Very good things had come of BL's relationship with Honda. The Triumph Acclaim featured a few dozen pages back had been a problem-free, and profitable, venture, and both partners were keen to renew their alliance.

So well before the Acclaim had time to turn stale, this car – based on the very latest Honda Civic – took its place. The decision was made to pension off the Triumph marque at this stage. Thanks to the excellent quality reputation enjoyed by the Acclaim, it was now felt that the more prestigious Rover brand could be extended down to a much smaller model.

Once again, the entire car was of Honda origination, and as the 213 it was complete with the Japanese company's 1.3-litre engine giving 71bhp. This time, though, Rover had a little more input on the design of the interior. It couldn't do much about the slightly cramped space, but it was able to influence the luxury feel and comfort of the seats and trim. In the 216 model, moreover, Rover's own 1.6-litre S Series engine was fitted (mated to a Honda five-speed

WHAT THEY SAID AT THE TIME

'The Rover 216 ... doesn't have any major flaws. It scores on handling, security and the right degree of upmarket appeal. Its main dismerit is an engine that gets rough when extended.'

Motor magazine in June 1985 on the £7,899 216 Vitesse.

This new small Rover took over from the successful Triumph Acclaim, and was deservedly popular from the start.

A Rover 216 EFi Vanden Plas from 1984, the range-topping model with Rover's own 1.6-litre fuel-injected engine – 213s used Honda motors.

gearbox like in the 213), and the fuel-injected edition gave a spirited 103bhp for the sporty Vitesse and plush Vanden Plas.

Quality was high enough for Honda to let Rover build a few of these for sale through its own dealers as the Honda Ballade – although it took the precaution of opening its own inspection centre in Swindon to make sure no 'Friday afternoon' specimens were released. The site served as the basis, eventually, for Honda's own British factory.

WHO LOVED IT?

Rover was chasing a mature demographic mostly spending their own money, so the 200 exuded quite a staid image. It was probably a much sounder prospect than Austin Rover's own Montego, and you'd always be better off with the Honda engine than the Rover one, to be frank.

Toyota MR2, 1984

Amazing, really, that it had taken so long: twelve years after the launch of the mid-engined Fiat X1/9 two-seater, Toyota came up with its first credible rival, the MR2, in 1984. Plenty of big-buck exotica used a similar layout because it offered weight distribution balance, with the heavy engine at the centre of the car. But, on affordable sports cars, it had been in decline, the ageing Fiat and the American Pontiac Fiero its only 1980s champions.

MR2 stood for Midships Recreational 2-seater and, by plundering its own corporate parts bin, Toyota had created a sure-fire winner: smooth, responsive twin-cam power matched to immaculate mid-engined poise was a combination nobody could touch in the affordable sports car arena. If flat cap-wearing traditionalists were suspicious of the slightly anodyne styling – not to mention Toyota's patchy pedigree as a maker of exciting cars – that was their problem.

One drive around the block in the MR2 (120mph, 30mpg) would convince anyone this was the ultimate in modern sports cars.

To keep its appeal broad, Toyota made sure it rode like a saloon, was acceptably quiet and had a comfortable driving position, not a low-slung sporty one that might have been off-putting. About the only black mark was the comparatively tight cockpit space.

From 1986 there was the T-bar version with removable roof sections,

WHAT THEY SAID AT THE TIME

'A sophisticated and extremely capable two-seat, mid-engine sports car that is a revelation to drive. Performance is excellent, as one might expect from an efficient, fuel-injected twin cam unit, and handling is nothing short of fantastic.'

Autocar magazine on the £9,939 MR2 in March 1985.

With traditional sports cars virtually an extinct species, the Toyota had the market largely to itself with the MR2.

Rapid and sure-footed, the MR2 impressed everybody. But the name, didn't work in French: M-R-Deux – say it quickly for a hidden double entendre …

WHO LOVED IT?

All Britain's old two-seater MGs and Triumphs had gone by the time the MR2 arrived so, apart from the Fiat X1/9 and a few kit cars, the MR2 was all there was on offer. Fortunately, it just happened to be a brilliant car to drive. And, being a Toyota, it was a trouble-free ownership experience too.

but Toyota never felt the need to import the hot 145bhp supercharged model to the UK because it would only run on unleaded petrol – and there wasn't much of that about in Britain in the mid-1980s!

The MR2 has inspired two more generations of mid-engined Toyotas and is already a sports car classic.

Not, perhaps, the daintiest of sports car to look at, the mid-mounting of the twin-cam engine was nonetheless highly effective.

Vauxhall Astra MkII, 1984

At around the time this startling new Astra appeared, with its curvaceous, aerodynamic body shape achieving an extremely low drag co-efficient of just 0.32, Vauxhall's fortunes themselves were riding on a gulf stream of prosperity.

The Cavalier was a huge hit, the Corsa was a decent weapon in the corporate armoury against Ford's Fiesta and the Austin Metro, and in January 1985 Vauxhall grabbed 20 per cent of the UK market, outselling BL/Austin Rover for the very first time.

The Astra simply augmented this success. The new styling was certainly radical, and took some

WHAT THEY SAID AT THE TIME

'Performance from a smooth and willing engine is up to scratch. Handling is safe and surefooted but the ride and road noise suppression could be better. Even in L guise it is as well equipped as a Ford Escort GL – and that makes it very good value.'

Motor magazine in March 1985 on the £6,544 Astra GL 1600S five-speed.

Vauxhall's brand new Astra took some getting used to, but it actually set the pace for aerodynamics among affordable family cars.

getting used to, but the rest of the car was largely carried over from the old model, with a revised front MacPherson strut/rear torsion beam axle suspension set-up, and a wide engine range from 1.2 to 1.8, added to which was a 1.6 diesel and a powerful petrol 2.0 in the rapid (134mph top, 0–60mph in 7.7 seconds) GTE hot hatchback.

In 1987, Vauxhall added a neat convertible to the range, available with a power-operated soft-top, which was somewhat more tempting than the related car it had launched the year before. This was the Belmont, basically an Astra but with a huge, saloon car-type boot sticking out at the back that sat very clumsily with the rest of the streamlined Astra profile.

The range lasted until the Astra MkIII of 1991, yet shortly after that, in 1995, these MkI cars would return to British showrooms, this time made in Korea and badged as the Daewoo Nexia, a name almost as ludicrous as Belmont.

Right: The Belmont, an Astra saloon, would never win any beauty contests, but served more conservative buyers well.

WHO LOVED IT?

Within a few months of its launch, Vauxhall had 40,000 Astra orders, was selling almost 7,000 cars a month, and had seen its new model immediately overtake the Austin Maestro in popularity. Ever more people were confident in turning to Vauxhall for cars that had really started to wallop market-leader Ford head-on for style and value.

Above: The MkI Astra convertible was the work of Italy's Bertone, and added a note of glamour to the humble Astra line-up.

Ford Granada/Scorpio, 1985

This kind of large executive car from a big, mainstream European brand, as opposed to a premium marque, is a thing of the past in the twenty-first century. Mercedes-Benz, Audi, Volvo, BMW and Lexus have squeezed them all out. But back in '85, when respect for the Ford Granada of the 1970s and '80s was still strong, this brand new model had real impact.

The car had gone the same way as the Sierra, replacing straight lines and boxy proportions with a sleek, undulating shape clearly fine-tuned in a wind tunnel. Also, like the Sierra over the Cortina, the new Granada eschewed the four-door saloon format for a five-door hatchback,

with an enormous tailgate leading on to masses of potential cargo space.

The Granada name was retained only for the British and Irish markets; everywhere else knew it as the 140mph Scorpio, although the top 2.8/2.9 V6 model was known here as the Granada Scorpio. It could be had with four-wheel drive, although the only transmission option with

that was a five-speed manual, which might have dismayed quite a few of the lazier executives likely to be taking the wheel. Other engines were 1.8 and 2.0 four-cylinders and a 2.4 V6, plus a 2.5 diesel.

This was the first range in the world to feature anti-lock brakes on every single model. And another minor innovation, perhaps not quite

WHO LOVED IT?

For the older generation of comfortable middle management choosing a large company car out of habit, this new Granada was a no-brainer, and it packed quite a lot of tech. But it would have been a rare private buyer who forked out for one, and even then it would likely be for the late estate model as a hugely capacious dual-purpose vehicle for long motorway drives.

Left: The Granada Scorpio found favour with a few police forces needing a powerful pursuit car for motorway duties.

Right: Ford put a lot of effort into its luxurious Granada – this is a late model Ghia – but it was an increasingly uphill battle to compete with premium marques.

so crucial to life and limb, was a pump-up adjustable lumber function on the seats, using a squeezable pneumatic rubber bulb.

All in all, a comfortable and capable large barge, but Ford's swan-song in its losing battle with the upmarket German brands.

WHAT THEY SAID AT THE TIME

'Make no mistake, the new Ford flagship is a fine car and, in some respects, it's a world-beater. It has an interior that is huge and truly sumptuous, a chassis that can stand comparison with the best at any price, and a host of clever design features.'

Motor magazine in June 1985 on the £15,550 Ford Granada Scorpio.

Mercedes-Benz 200–300, 1985

At the time, the wider car market – the non-Mercedes-owning stratum, that is – was maybe a little indifferent to this brand new W124 Series: more of the same from Stuttgart, unadventurous and yet reassuringly expensive.

In retrospect, though, it can be seen as one of the last of the traditionally built Benzes. In those days, you got what you paid for and the big price premium was for a car with exemplary build quality and now-legendary durability, which could rack up anything between 250,000 and 300,000 miles and still seem like new. The excellent multi-link rear suspension was shared with the 190.

This was the mainstay of the range, the mid-market Merc, with a choice of four-door saloon, five-door estate and two-door coupé or convertible bodywork, and under the bonnet

The brand new mid-range Mercedes was all that owners could ask for in terms of engineering integrity, restrained style and unbreakable durability.

WHO LOVED IT?

These high quality cars were calculated to appeal to the core Mercedes-Benz customer base, while gradually expanding the appeal of the marque to new customers. Impressively, more than 2.5 million were sold and it was rightly popular in the UK as elsewhere. Quality on subsequent cars, though, nosedived, as Mercedes, ill-advisedly, sought to scrimp on manufacturing costs.

WHAT THEY SAID AT THE TIME

'The 300E is one of few four-seater saloons that will top 140mph, quite a feat for any 3-litre machine, and it will do this with ease, even with Mercedes' excellent four-speed automatic gearbox.'

Autocar in October 1985 on the £17,840 300E.

This coupé body style added sophisticated styling to the W124's sound basic tenets, and was a quick car with the 3.0-litre 24-valve straight-six engine.

everything from a meagre 2.0 petrol engine to a 260bhp 24-valve 3.0 straight-six, by way of the marque's usual unburstable diesels and turbo diesels. There was also a very rare 500E, with a loony Porsche-devised V8 engine transplant. Most came as autos and there was now a four-wheel drive option on the 300E 4MATIC estate – at a massive extra cost of six grand!

The cars still had some distinctive features, mind you, such as a foot-operated parking brake and a smaller door mirror on the passenger side to reduce overall width. And you couldn't fail to be well pleased with the interior which, while sober in its dashboard design and layout, came with very comfortable seats and a hushed ambience closed off from the hectic world beyond those electric windows.

Colour-coded credentials: all the green parts were easily recyclable, while the blue catalytic converter could be reprocessed.

Peugeot 309, 1985

A roomy family hatchback with a particularly good ride quality, this Peugeot model had nimble handling and a wide roster of engines to select from, including a 1.9-litre diesel. These came with three- and five-door bodywork, and the former provided the capable basis for the fiery 309 GTi, with the same 1.9-litre fuel-injected engine as the large-engined 205, for which it was just about the equal in terms of fun and road-holding.

Despite all that, the 309 was an oddity in the Peugeot range. It seemed that by rounding off its title with a '9' instead of a '5' they were signifying that the car really didn't belong in the line-up.

In truth, the 309 contained the last standalone vestiges of Talbot, a marque name introduced in 1979 and fizzling out, for cars at least, in 1986. The 309 had been designed in Britain as a replacement for the largely unloved Talbot Horizon, a second-rate Golf competitor, but at the eleventh hour Talbot owner Peugeot changed its mind, and launched the car under its own, well-regarded nameplate. It had already insisted that the car use door panels

WHO LOVED IT?

The 309 wasn't particularly handsome, and was underrated for its abilities, but did reasonably well over its seven-year stint in showrooms, selling over 800,000 examples. Buyers wisely opted, in the main, for the five-door. What it did do was build up a good customer base for its successor, the excellent Peugeot 306, which squared up manfully to the dominant Golf, Astra and Escort.

The 309 was developed as a Talbot but reached customers wearing Peugeot badges; this is the fiesty SR Injection five-door.

WHAT THEY SAID AT THE TIME

'Performance and handling are very rewarding attributes, and similarly this fuel-injected 1.6-litre engine is also light on fuel. Inside there's an inviting driving position, light controls with the exception of steering (heavy) and throttle (too light), but despite these faults the Peugeot does not fail to impress as an enthusiastic driver's car.'

Autocar magazine in November 1986 on the £8,495 309 SR Injection.

from the 205 to save money, and all the power units were Peugeot's own anyway.

So, in the Peugeot catalogue, it slotted in between the 205 supermini and the long-serving 305 saloon.

Still, all the right-hand drive cars were built in Coventry in the former Rootes/Hillman/Chrysler/Talbot plant, making this the first of four Peugeots that would be built on British soil.

The performance pick of the 309 range was this riotously enjoyable GTi – just as exhilarating as its 205 equivalent.

1980s Car Culture

Britain's allegiance to Ford cars in the 1980s was absolutely unshakeable. In a large majority of the years between 1980 and 1989 inclusive, the company's Escort, Fiesta, Cortina and/or Sierra would hog the top three spots in the annual sales charts, the only interlopers being (twice apiece) the Austin Metro and Vauxhall Cavalier.

The Essex-based giant hardly made a secret of its winning ways. Its range covered all bases, and there was a vast choice of engine and trim levels. Radical technology was avoided but the latest styling trends were followed – and often set – assiduously. Ford tended to introduce spin-off models after listening to customer demands, such as conventional saloon versions of popular hatchbacks, like the Orion and Sierra Sapphire. And, finally, its marketing was bold, simple and relentlessly emphasised value.

Plus, of course, you could feel quite patriotic about buying a Ford, because most of what it sold was built in

The last CORTINA
1962-1982

Goodbye, old friend: smiles all round as the very last Cortina is completed at Ford's Dagenham factory, but its successor the Sierra was to have a bumpy ride with company car buyers.

Ford's 1984 chart-toppers included the Escort (at the back), the Orion (left) and the fully updated Fiesta, all cars much loved by British buyers.

Above: New and used cars were still bought from traditional dealers; this is Dutton Forshaw on London's Edgware Road in about 1986, selling new Vauxhalls and second-hand examples of everything from Range Rovers to Golf GTis.

Right: Austin Rover and Asda teamed up in 1986 to try selling new cars in supermarkets, but the experiment wasn't a success.

either Dagenham or Merseyside. That was taken as a given at the time but today, of course, not one single Ford vehicle is manufactured in the UK.

There was not a little nationalistic fervour in our attachment to the Austin Metro, although it also happened to be quite a good (but by no means the best) 'supermini' small car. The desperate plight of British Leyland in the 1970s was an almost nightly feature of news programmes and, despite the country's dwindling patience with the terrible industrial relations in the company, we seemed willing to get behind the firm one more time to make the Metro a hit and, with a little more reluctance, the later and larger Maestro and Montego.

The most remarkable progress in the '80s, though, was made by the once also-ran Vauxhall.

The catalyst was its all-new Cavalier of 1981. It was, quite simply, an all-round excellent car for

Prime Minister Margaret Thatcher gets the low-down on car-making at Nissan's Sunderland factory in 1986 as Japanese manufacturers changed the shape of the British car industry.

Strongman Geoff Capes gives a lift to the new Volkswagen Polo in 1983 – smaller, lighter cars being the way the new car market was heading.

Dutton Cars
Europe's leading kit manufacturer

its purpose, which was to tempt the all-important fleet managers who bought Britain's company cars.

This coterie of deeply conservative people had to balance the attraction of the 'perk' with the cost to their companies of the purchase *and* the anticipated running costs. For years, the Ford Cortina had ruled the roost because it was quite a big car that could be bought in bulk quantities at a discounted price; its running gear was simple and, when Cortinas did go wrong, they were cheap to mend.

Now fleet buyers were hearing about the upcoming Ford Sierra. And they weren't liking it much. The aerodynamic styling was too radical and the old Cortina engine and drivetrain was falling behind the times compared to the latest, well-proven front-wheel drive cars from Volkswagen and Peugeot.

The Cavalier, then, hit the spot. Front-wheel drive for safe road-holding, a choice of neat saloon or hatchback bodies, thrifty engines, and made in England. And it certainly helped that the car garnered glowing reports from motoring journalists.

The company car was a crucial part of the pay package for hundreds of thousands of 1980s white-collar workers. At the time, inflation was rampant, and one way to keep workers happy was to throw in a car as a 'benefit in kind' that could really help make the most of their cash salaries. Company directors and some high-paid employees were required to pay tax on their executive models and limousines, but for many people on average incomes, a 'firm's car' was a motivating, no-strings freebie.

The end of this state of affairs was signalled in 1983, when the Treasury came up with 'tax break' levels for new cars in bands up to 1.3 litres, from 1.3 to 1.8 litres, and 1.8 litres and above with the assault on the wallet increasing with each step. And it was here that the Cavalier really scored because Vauxhall had already launched a 1796cc fuel-injected petrol engine in 1982, at the same time as adding a superb 1.6 litre diesel engine option. Cavalier sales fair exploded, and the company was quick to exploit its new-found popularity with its new Nova and Astra models. Suddenly, it really was a hot rival to market-leader Ford.

So … here are the figures for the top ten single best-selling cars in the UK between 1980 and 1989.

Left: If you wanted a fun car on the cheap and were a little bit handy with the toolbox then a kit car was one way to go. This is the cover of market leader Dutton's brochure in 1983.

Right: If you owned a pleasant suburban house, and a comfy Volvo 340, then an electric garage door operated by remote control could only enhance your 1980s lifestyle!

Mobile phones were the new must-haves of the time, and if you didn't want to trudge around with a brick-like handset and heavy, car battery-type power source then Renault could offer you a 'cellular telephone' plumbed into your new car, such as this 25 in 1987.

No. 1: Ford Escort, 1,607,999 registered; No. 2: Ford Fiesta, 1,273,689 registered; No. 3: Vauxhall Cavalier, 1,007,866 registered; No. 4: Ford Sierra, 979,379 registered; No. 5: Austin Metro, 913,336 registered; No. 6: Vauxhall Astra, 654,933 registered; No. 7: Ford Cortina, 497,706 registered; No. 8: Ford Orion, 384,381 registered; No. 9: Vauxhall Nova, 360,829 registered; and No. 10: Austin Maestro, 324,125 registered. Points of interest are that the Cortina was only around for three years at the start, the Ford Orion was really an Escort with a boot, effectively putting the chart-topper even further ahead of the pack, and the only 100 per cent imported car

was the Nova – the others were either all-British or mostly manufactured here.

During the 1980s, and well before the dawn of the Internet age, new cars were still bought from local dealers, and the big manufacturers had chains of independent local agents – many of them old-established family businesses – that often ran into the thousands of outlets.

Austin Rover, in 1986, tried selling its cars through Asda supermarkets (the first being in Poplar, East London), but the venture was short-lived and unsuccessful. Meanwhile, by 1982 it was estimated that some 2 per cent of all new cars sold were 'grey' imports – brand new, right-hand drive models that had actually been delivered to countries like Belgium and Ireland before coming to the UK, and sold at prices considerably lower than those charged by UK importers. In many cases this highlighted how much more, on average, British drivers were expected to pay for new cars.

But what if you couldn't really afford a new car?

One way was to purchase a Lada, a Škoda or an FSO. These cars were all from countries behind the Soviet Bloc Iron Curtain, and were sold at extremely low prices in the UK – the sort of money that many might spend instead on a second-hand car. For a while, and despite their often poor quality, these bargain-basement machines did quite well.

If you did want a used motor then, apart from car lots and the second-hand car selection at franchised dealers, you'd probably find what you wanted from small ads in your local newspaper, or in cheap and cheerful small ad rags like *Exchange & Mart* or *Thames Valley Trader*, later to become *Auto Trader*. Fly-by-night car dealers abounded as the used-car market boomed following the massive rise in car ownership of the 1960s and '70s, and every week on TV we were treated to the misadventures of one such individual, Arthur Daley, in the hit comedy-action show *Minder*. Sawdust in the gearbox to disguise wear and write-offs cunningly welded-up and resprayed littered the plots, for sure, but it was a bit too close to reality for comfort.

Traditional small sports cars had all but vanished by the start of the decade, as MGs and Triumphs faced the axe. If you had the money then you might have got your driving kicks from a hot hatchback, but for those who still wanted wind-in-the-hair exhilaration, there was a second coming of the kit car. Products like the Dutton Phaeton, Caterham 7 and Marlin recycled the innards of MoT-failure Fords, while the Midas and GTM did the same with Minis and the Nova, and various beach buggies put new life into rusted-out Volkswagen Beetles. The popularity of

Estate of the nation: Liberal Party leader between 1976 and 1988, David Steel was an avid car fan, using this unusual Lynx Eventer estate conversion of the Jaguar XJS as his everyday drive.

these cars also brought well-known 'component' marques like Ginetta and Marcos back to life.

Classic cars, and the burgeoning interest around them, was another 1980s phenomenon, with an explosion of magazines, owners' clubs, exhibitions and firms specialising in restoration or remaking hard-to-find parts. Values of these cars began to rise fast, and there was money to be made, but the investment bubble burst in 1989, and quite a few speculators got their fingers burnt.

It was classics that tended to feature in many memorable 'car' movies of these years, such as the (replica) Ferrari 250 California in *Ferris Bueller's Day Off*, the Hudson Hornet in *Driving Miss Daisy*, Tucker Torpedo in *Tucker: The Man and His Dream*, the Cadillac 62 in *Tin Men*, the Plymouth Fury in *Christine* and the Jaguar Mk2 in *Withnail and I*. Something more contemporary in the 1987 007 epic *The Living Daylights* was also a cheering cinematic sight – the return of Aston Martin, with a new V8, as James Bond's ride.

Meanwhile, on the small screen, American TV again provided some of the iconic cars of the '80s, with the talking KITT (a Pontiac Firebird) in *Knight Rider*, the white Ferrari Testarossa in *Miami Vice*, and the A-Team's GMC van and Chevrolet Corvette. British producers gave us a Reliant van in *Only Fools and Horses* and an Austin Maestro in *Brookside*.

On the roads of Britain, the eagle-eyed could pick out something new in 1983: the first change in the system

Jeff Bridges as Preston Tucker in the 1988 biopic *Tucker: The Man and His Dream*, which told the tale of the would-be car industry buccaneer and his thwarting by an apprehensive Detroit establishment.

David Hasselhoff in hit US TV adventure series *Knight Rider*, sitting in KITT, the all-powerful Pontiac Firebird with which he had an ongoing dialogue.

For most of us, the mid-1980s was a time to get used to the new 'prefix' number plate system, but for Scouse joker and golf addict Jimmy Tarbuck it was a time to transfer his cherished registration on to his latest Merc, a 560 SEC.

of registration numbers since 1963. Having used up all the available combinations of three-letter area codes, up to three digits, and a single letter at the end to indicate the issuing year (running from July to August), the Driver & Vehicle Licensing Centre in Swansea turned the layout back to front. Henceforth, and starting with the new A-registrations beginning 1 August 1983, the year identifying letter would be at the start, followed by the digits and then the three-letter area code. It would be another twenty years before they had to think again, and in the interim the DVLC got into the 'personal' plates business in 1989 when it began to market a selection of so-called desirable, unissued registration numbers to anyone prepared to pay for them.

Rover 800, 1985

The 800 was a radical change for Rover's biggest and most prestigious model. The outgoing SD1 was a handsome, rear-drive hatchback with a powerful V8 engine in its most opulent form, but this new car came only as a four-door saloon, and heading the range was a 2.5-litre V6.

What's more, this engine was provided by Honda, the Japanese manufacturer with whom Austin Rover co-designed the car. The groundbreaking joint venture aimed to give the partners just the vehicle they each needed – Rover its replacement for the creaky SD1, and Honda an impressive sedan to tackle its Japanese counterparts in the crucial North American market.

The basic metal architecture was identical to save on development costs, and it was agreed Honda would produce the 2.5-litre V6 engines for the top models in both ranges; Rover's would be called the 800 Series, and Honda's car the Legend. From there, the pair diverged, with entirely different outer panels and interiors, and Rover also offered a four-cylinder model with its

Above: There was much residual affection for the older SD1, so Rover hastily added a similarly versatile 800 Fastback, this being the sportiest Vitesse derivative.

Left: The pinnacle of the 800 range was occupied by the sumptuously appointed Sterling, with a 2.5 and later 2.7 Honda V6 engine.

own, responsive M Series power units to tempt a wider range of business customers in the UK and Europe.

The Legend did well, in the US especially. But when Rover tried to sell its 800 there, the British version bombed, let down by poor build quality and patchy reliability like several British Leyland cars before it. Added to which, the styling was fairly anonymous.

Nevertheless, an 820 or 825 (soon replaced by the 827 whose 2.7 engine gave a much smoother performance) were comfortable, well-equipped large cars with a typically light, Japanese quality to their steering and transmission. They even added an alternative five-door Fastback body for those who sorely missed the versatility of the old SD1.

WHAT THEY SAID AT THE TIME

'All told, the 820 Si emerges as the sensible choice in the Rover 800 range. The 820 is better balanced than the Sterling, with crisper steering and better suspension control. Cabin has class and is well planned. Equipment levels high.'

Motor magazine in November 1986 on the £13,247 820 Si.

WHO LOVED IT?

Business people who might otherwise have bought a Ford Granada or Vauxhall Carlton, but were drawn by the more upmarket Rover aura; the top 800 Sterling had a largely hand-finished interior, with Connolly leather upholstery and air-conditioning. As the years rolled by, and with several revamps and facelifts, the 800 continued to sell in respectable numbers.

The interior of the Rover 820 was comfortable and spacious, if a touch plasticky in a more typically Japanese fashion.

Saab 9000, 1985

The first all-new Saab for many a long year was also, like the Rover on the previous spread, a co-production. In this case, the Swedes got together with Italian giant Fiat to pool costs. That meant the highly impressive 9000 executive car used the 'Type Four' body/chassis structure that could also be found, unseen, underpinning the Fiat Croma, Alfa Romeo 164 and Lancia Thema.

The Saab was the second of the quartet to be launched, after the Lancia. The very first version on offer was the Saab 9000 Turbo, which could reach 145mph thanks to its turbocharged 2.0-litre, four-cylinder, 16-valve engine with 175bhp on tap, and an excellent turbo installation that all but curtailed lag thanks to carefully set ignition and fuel injection electronics. The car could hit 60mph from rest in 7.4 seconds.

It had superior construction to its sisters, with substantial side impact bars in its doors, and an exceptionally safe and pleasant interior, with seats that set the benchmark for comfort and support. The dashboard was angled towards the driver with clear, logical controls, and the ignition key was positioned between the seats, just like on the 900.

Within a few months, there was a non-turbo model too, but this was still a 127mph car, with its 130bhp, rising to 150bhp when the engine size was boosted to 2.3 litres in 1989.

WHAT THEY SAID AT THE TIME

'Big hatchback in overtly aero shell, excellent performer in traditional turbo style, with very noticeable step in power delivery but perfectly civilised in starting, driveaway and quietness if not hurried. Well equipped but expensive even by Saab standards.'

Autocar in October 1985 on the £15,995 9000 Turbo.

The Saab 9000 Turbo was one of the best-built executive cars around, more than capable of withstanding a tough Swedish winter.

These superior cars would usher in Saab's golden era as credible rivals to German premium marques, always relying on relatively modest engines, excellent safety systems and plenty of thoughtful details to give them an edge.

WHO LOVED IT?

This was the thinking person's choice as an executive car that could cover huge mileages with secure road manners and brilliant comfort, and highly satisfying performance. It turned Saab into a contender well beyond its core constituent of middle-class professionals like architects, doctors and solicitors.

The 9000 was a handsome car, thanks to masterful styling input from Italy's Giugiaro on the five-door hatchback body.

Within, the Saab shared its basic architecture with the Fiat Croma, Lancia Thema and Alfa Romeo 164 … only it was much, much better made.

Seat Ibiza, 1985

Just to make sure everyone recognised this was a wholly Spanish car, it bore the name of a popular holiday destination in the Med. It certainly needed to stand out in the crowded supermini market, especially since Seat, as a marque, was totally new to the UK market.

For several decades, state-owned Seat had built Fiat cars under licence, but the relationship had soured and now the Spanish had decided to create their own cars from scratch. Well, almost from scratch; the Ibiza used some parts such as suspension from the Fiat Strada-based Seat Ronda, and the smallest engine on offer was identical to that in the Fiat/Seat Panda.

The company called on some impressive consultants for expertise. Italy's Giugiaro did the neat styling; Germany's Porsche designed a range of 1.2 and 1.5 four-cylinder engines, with five-speed manual gearboxes, and allowed Seat to label them 'System Porsche' even though they were no great shakes in terms of mechanical smoothness; and Karmann, also German, provided the know-how for tooling up to manufacture the car.

Considering it was an all-new car from an unknown brand, British sales made a healthy start, no doubt

WHAT THEY SAID AT THE TIME

'Performance and fuel consumption are well up to modern standards, but overall mechanical refinement is not that impressive when compared with the competition.'
Autocar magazine in October 1985 on the £5,569 Ibiza 1.5GLX three-door.

The trim lines of the Seat Ibiza, which was the first car produced from the ground up by the ambitious Spanish company.

Ramsgate, Kent, in 1985, and the first few truckloads of right-hand drive Ibizas begin their onward journey to a brand new dealer network.

WHO LOVED IT?

Buying an Ibiza was likely to be a decision of the rational head rather than the racing heart and in that context, with considerations of price, finance, dealer proximity and metal-for-the-money, it made sense. Actually, it wasn't bad to drive and the interior space certainly was a boon.

It was roomy inside an Ibiza but the dashboard looked a bit cheap and nasty; refinement was poor, too, but prices were competitive.

helped by keen pricing. The Ibiza, with either three or five doors, had a particularly roomy cabin.

This and the Malaga saloon, however, would be the first and last independently created Seats, as in 1986 Volkswagen took a controlling interest in the company. This meant that the next-generation Ibiza would be entirely Volkswagen-based, and frankly all the better for it.

Jaguar XJ6, 1986

Once Jaguar was sold off from British Leyland in a hugely successful Stock Market flotation in 1984, it could finally bring its all-new saloon car to market in the way it saw fit

Designers and engineers had been occupied with various aspects of this impressive executive model since as long ago as 1972 but the various crises troubling either the company's ultimate owner or the economy in general had seen it postponed countless times.

Right: Some opulent versions of the new Jag adopted the former Daimler name of Sovereign to set them apart.

Below: The all-new Jaguar's styling was an evolution of the original XJ6 dating back to 1968, and it looked very tasteful indeed.

WHO LOVED IT?

Jaguar was constantly battling quality issues, many of them resulting from outdated factory facilities, so the new XJ40 cars had a fair few teething problems. And the totally new Lexus LS400 of 1990 set a formidably high new benchmark for customer satisfaction. But these things didn't impinge too deeply on sales both at home and abroad. Because, if you liked Jaguar's unique cocktail of refinement, style and performance, there was still nothing else quite like it.

SOVEREIGN

Acres of finely crafted leather and a gorgeous walnut dashboard ensured the interior of the 'XJ40' wouldn't dismay traditionalists.

Finally here it was, and in place of the slender curves and chrome accents was a more angular car with more prominent bumpers, but still in an entirely familiar overall shape.

The venerable XK engine, which had served Jaguar cars well since 1948, was finally ousted by all-new AJ6 six-cylinder power units in 2.9- and 3.6-litre sizes, with either Getrag five-speed manual or ZF four-speed automatic transmission.

The road manners and ride comfort were every inch as accomplished as you'd expect from Jag and, because the car was lighter and more aerodynamically accomplished, it felt considerably more nimble. However, even Jaguar couldn't resist the fads of the time, and so until 1990 all of these so-called 'XJ40' cars had digital instruments that no-one really liked replaced by analogue items at that point. And, imposing though it looked, it wasn't terribly spacious inside, although the cabin ambience with its swathes of leather and walnut or rosewood veneer was something else compared to the colourless interior environments offered by Mercedes and BMW.

Meanwhile, the old and much-loved XJ12 Series III continued to be built alongside the XJ40 until 1993 when Jaguar had finally worked out a way to install its superb 6.0-litre V12 engine in the new structure.

WHAT THEY SAID AT THE TIME

'Arguably the most important launch of 1986, the new XJ6 may not look significantly different from its predecessor. Don't be fooled: it's a completely new car from the ground up with a nearly magical ride and handling compromise.'
Autocar magazine in October 1986 on the £18,495 XJ6 3.6.

Nissan Bluebird, 1986

If you've seen one of these boxy looking saloons or hatchbacks of late then it's most likely to have been in the thick of the action on the banger racing circuit. Fifteen or twenty years ago, they were ubiquitous as minicabs all over the country, reeking of Magic Tree and with the upholstery wearing thin.

The Bluebird was always a tough car, with bodywork in particular whose steel was uncommonly resistant to corrosion and engines that could take any amount of abuse.

This particular example of the several cars to have worn the Bluebird badge in Britain was, perhaps, one of the least thrilling cars launched in 1986. It was front-wheel drive with a five-speed gearbox, almost always with power steering, and could be had as an estate or with a 2.0 diesel engine in addition to the 1.6, 1.8 and 2.0 petrol motors.

But it was a highly significant car. It was the first to go into production in Sunderland at Nissan's new UK factory there, and is the cornerstone upon which this phenomenally productive plant was built. At first, it was mostly bolted together from imported parts, by a workforce still learning the ropes. But as they proved themselves adept at high quality work, the local content level very quickly rose as more

The new shape of the British car industry: just finished Bluebird Executives coming off the Nissan production line in Sunderland.

WHAT THEY SAID AT THE TIME

'Equipment levels are very high in typical Japanese fashion, and as such the car looks good value for money. The rather square proportions do mean that it is a convenient shape, and the folding rear seat backrests add a further dimension to the load capacity. There is little to criticise about this newcomer.'

Autocar magazine in August 1986 on the £10,345 Bluebird ZX Turbo.

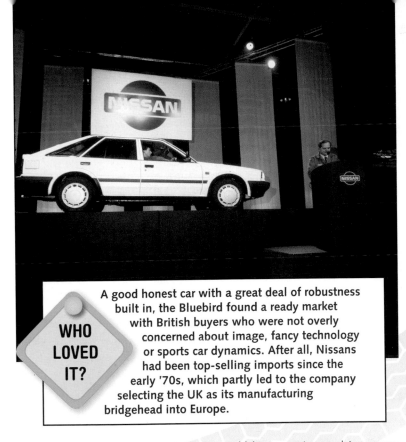

WHO LOVED IT?

A good honest car with a great deal of robustness built in, the Bluebird found a ready market with British buyers who were not overly concerned about image, fancy technology or sports car dynamics. After all, Nissans had been top-selling imports since the early '70s, which partly led to the company selecting the UK as its manufacturing bridgehead into Europe.

and more of the cars were actually manufactured here. The feature-rich Executive model featured such niceties as English Connolly leather upholstery, a body kit, air-con and alloy wheels, although it would have scant appeal to anyone contemplating a BMW or a Merc.

You can pay homage to the very first British Bluebird on permanent display at the Sunderland Museum and Winter Gardens.

Above left: The very first car made by Nissan in Britain takes centre stage in an event at the Washington plant, which today is one of Europe's most productive.

Above: The first Tyne and Wear-made Bluebird for export gets a glowing send-off from Tory minister Lord Young in 1986.

Vauxhall Carlton, 1986

Who would have thought that Vauxhall's Carlton, extremely decent large saloon that it was, would give rise to one of the most extraordinary performance cars of the 1980s? The Lotus Carlton, with its trick 3.6-litre engine and twin turbochargers, generated an amazing 377bhp. This abundant power could propel it to 175mph, making it the fastest four-door production saloon of all time (at the time). A comprehensive aerodynamic package and huge alloy wheels were required, along with massive brakes. It was a getaway driver's dream, yet surprisingly easy and safe to drive.

It cost £48,000 and by-hand production was strictly limited, but the Carlton GSi 3000 24-valve cost substantially less and yet still

WHO LOVED IT?

If you weren't too bothered about brands, and wanted a relaxed and spacious car that could cruise happily all day, at high speed when required, only the smallest-engined Carlton might disappoint. The estates were cavernous, and a lot less money than an equivalent Volvo 740.

Below: The Lotus Carlton was once the fastest four-door production car on this planet, its bespoke engine powering it to 175mph.

Left: The Carlton flew the flag for Vauxhall in the large saloon sector, and was a very good car for all the brand's humble associations.

'Performance is enough to give the Carlton's rivals a good run for the money. Its chassis is also finely tuned to match. Here, in particular, the 3000 GSi excels. Certainly likely to cause a stir in the company car park with its sporty looks, but not overt enough to upset the managing director.'

Autocar magazine in April 1987 on the £18,264 Carlton 3000 GSi.

The Carlton GSi was also a storming performance express, capable of 147mph thanks to its 24-valve 3.0-litre straight-six engine.

had a brilliant chassis, could hit 147mph and came fully loaded. The 12-valve model was only slightly less accomplished.

More attainable still were the other saloons and estates, with 1.8 and 2.0 fours or a 2.6 V6, along with a rather less scintillating 2.3 diesel (a much better turbo diesel arrived only in the 1990s).

As conservative, rear-drive large cars of the old school, Carltons were big on comfort and space, and built – by Opel for Vauxhall – like tanks. The refined four-speed automatic was the transmission to opt for, rather than the indifferent five-speed manual. Yet the handling was always good. Like its arch-enemy the Granada, the Carlton was

beginning to feel the heat from other German and Japanese models with premium badges, so its prospects were slowly dwindling. Nevertheless, Vauxhall at this time aimed even higher by adding the Carlton-based Senator in 1987, yet another excellent model that just fell short of the aspirational heartland of 1980s executive car buyers.

Citroën AX, 1987

Excellent aerodynamics and a ruthless emphasis on lightness – the steel panels were individually as thin as they needed to be for the load they bore, while the tailgate was plastic, and the most basic car weighed just 640kg – made the AX a standard-bearer for economical motoring. To prove it, in 1989, a 1.3-litre model was driven from Dover to Barcelona and over the 1,000-mile journey managed an average 100mpg.

Its role was to replace the Visa and LN models simultaneously as Citroën's distinctive take on the supermini. The platform of the car was entirely fresh, and there was initially a choice of 1.0, 1.1 and 1.3 litre engines, power ranging from 45bhp to 65bhp, with a 1.4 diesel soon afterwards. In 1988 came the cool-looking AX GT, with an 85bhp 1.3 engine and a very eager appetite for acceleration and cornering thanks to a stiffened incarnation of the AX's usually long-travel all-round independent suspension.

The very last AX, a special edition entitled the Spree, drives into the sunset…leaving the perky AX legacy intact in the replacement Saxo.

The Citroën AX would prove enormously popular because it offered miserly fuel economy with great driving verve.

Citroën design details abounded, such as the partly enclosed rear wheels, and the interior contained an unusually large number of storage compartments, including the memorable recesses in the two front doors that could each take a 2.0-litre water or soft drinks bottle. Despite the tight wheelbase, it was pretty roomy for such a pint-sized vehicle, and the optional five-door guise added in 1987 provided yet more versatility.

It was built for twelve years, and was such a well-resolved answer to thrifty yet enjoyable motoring that it formed the basis of both the subsequent Citroën Saxo and Peugeot 106.

WHAT THEY SAID AT THE TIME

'What lets the AX down is an almost inevitable penalty of its class-leading lightness. It is not a quiet car, with intrusive tyre roar and a high degree of noise when its 1.1-litre engine is being used hard.'

Autocar magazine in August 1988 on the £6,358 AX 11 TRE five-door.

One of the keynotes of the original AX's interior was its clever storage units, including these big, bottle-friendly door nacelles.

WHO LOVED IT?

With over 2.4 million examples sold, here was another very popular small car from France. It appealed to British drivers as both a neat city machine for singletons, an ideal first car with low insurance premiums, and a low-cost runabout for the retired brigade.

Volvo 480ES, 1987

Volvos had always been distinctive cars but this sporty three-door model really was quite different from anything else around – a hybrid coupé-hatchback mixing some old Volvo keynotes with a whole bunch of aspects that were entirely new to the Swedish marque.

It was, for instance, the first Volvo with front-wheel drive and a transversely mounted engine. It remains Volvo's only car ever to feature flip-up headlights, and no car from the firm had ever boasted such sophisticated electronics. Meanwhile, the unusual frameless glass hatchback revived a signature feature from Volvo's last vaguely sporty offering, the 1800ES.

There were some 18 months between the 480ES's unveiling in 1985 and its arrival in British showrooms in 1987. The car was built in Holland and, although it was intended to appeal to American buyers, unprofitable currency exchange rates meant it was never exported there. Instead, the car's chassis formed the basis of the more conventional 440 and 460 saloons and hatchbacks.

The car performed strongly thanks to its Renault-based but Porsche-modified engine, and went round corners safely on its suspension system refined by Lotus. It was even more sparkling in Turbo form, with 120bhp over 109 and much more flexible torque for mid-range

The pop-up headlights were just one snappy feature of the Volvo 480ES that set it apart from the crowd.

144

urge. Later on, and after catalytic converters were fitted to comply with tighter emissions laws, a 2.0-litre engine was called for to keep performance up to scratch.

The car was comfortable and the facia was unusually towering, although one criticism was the cabin's closed-in gloominess. A convertible, which would have sorted that out, was often promised but in the end never made production.

The car was supposed to start an adventurous new era for Volvo, hence Porsche input on the engine and Lotus's influence on the handling.

WHAT THEY SAID AT THE TIME

'Volvo has managed to combine excellent road manners with a very pliant ride, making the 480ES a comfortable long-distance car. Both [steering] wheel and seat have plenty of adjustment inbuilt.'

Autocar magazine in June 1987 on the £11,495 480ES.

WHO LOVED IT?

Sadly, the central electronics 'brain' in the car was a bit too ambitious for Volvo, and the car was prone to water leaks, so it took a few years for 480ESs to become reliable. Those later cars were much loved by their owners, offering a uniquely Nordic combination of style and versatility. As only some 80,000 examples were made, it will surely become a collector's piece.

BMW 5 Series MKIII, 1988

Aficionados of the marque rate this as one of the finest BMW sports saloons ever. They know it as the E34, its internal company development code.

These folk have an old-school love of the four round, uncovered headlights and the elegant and restrained Bavarian styling which mark the car out as a beacon of good taste. This was BMW evolution at its slow-cooked best, and it would be around in various forms, the fabled M5 and an estate included, until 1995.

Under the bonnet, of course, was a selection of the company's superb straight-six engines. Even the base 129bhp 2.0 was a paragon of smoothness and refinement, either with five-speed manual or four-speed automatic transmission. The 170bhp 2.5 was a little so-so in terms of mid-range performance, but the 3.0 and especially the 211bhp 3.5-litre editions made these cars the finest

sports saloons on the planet. The taut ride allied to supple absorption of nasty shocks from the road surface was a balance that BMW alone seemed to get spot-on at the time. Much later would come a 1.8 four-cylinder unit, and a pair of V8s, but it's these sixes that really do it for BMW connoisseurs.

The interior ambience was sophisticated, beautifully assembled and comfortable, with perhaps the lone criticism being the tight passenger space in the back.

This was also an uncommonly safe car, with all-round anti-lock brakes and driver and passenger airbags on

every model, allied to a rigid, high quality structure and body shell that would stand up well in a shunt.

WHAT THEY SAID AT THE TIME

'The best production saloon car made. It isn't simply that it does so many things so well but the way all the elements hang together to make an effective, cohesive whole. When it comes to ride and handling, however, the 535i sets the standard.'

Autocar magazine in May 1988 on the £25,391 535i SE.

A BMW 525i Sport, one of the excellent range of executive cars that garnered ecstatic reviews from critics and customers.

WHO LOVED IT?

BMW drivers had started to gain their reputation for impatience and arrogance at the time, one that was partly true in the press-ahead 1980s before the 'Black Monday' shares crash. But this was a logical choice for anyone seeking a long-distance driver that was comfortable, safe and fun. Plus, as survey after survey proved, it was very well built and robust, meaning many of the 1.2 million made would enjoy a long life.

M ⊛ RE 8140 ⊙

Above: Taut handling and the suspension's ability to smooth out surface imperfections gave the new 5 Series peerless road manners for a sports saloon.

Left: The 5 Series generated its own estate spin-off, the Touring, with this novel tailgate featuring an independently opening rear window for easy access to light items.

Peugeot 405, 1988

We would not have realised it at the time but the 405 would become something of a global phenomenon in its idiosyncratic way. It was, of course, designed and engineered in France but the elegant styling, with highly effective aerodynamics, was the creation of Italy's famed design house Pininfarina.

But, beyond its home borders, one of the biggest markets for the 405 was Argentina, where about a fifth of the 2.5 million examples manufactured were sold. And even today, it continues as one of the most popular cars in Iran, where versions modified for local conditions are still

being churned out. And not only that but the 405 was also produced in Coventry, here in the UK.

It was a handsome car and also a strong one, with very good road manners and a forgiving ride. Engines, for the UK, ranged from 1.6 to 1.9 petrol and a 1.9-litre diesel; equipped with the 90bhp 1.8 turbo diesel a 405 became a very rapid yet pleasingly economical choice. Still, the ultimate performance model was the Mi16, with a 166bhp twin-camshaft petrol engine. Its acceleration was electric, taking 8.2 seconds to hit 60mph, and with the optional four-wheel drive

WHAT THEY SAID AT THE TIME

'The 1.9-litre all-alloy engine kicks out a healthy 125bhp. Equipped with electronic fuel injection, this fine powerplant is responsive, smooth and flexible. But it is not the engine that makes the 405 the star of the class; it is the chassis. Peugeot engineers have achieved ride and handling of rare ability.'

Autocar magazine in March 1988 on the £10,455 405 SRi saloon.

Pininfarina's clean styling and an expertly balanced front-wheel drive layout were combined in the Peugeot 405.

WHO LOVED IT?

Customers and critics alike were unanimous in their praise for the car, and having it built in this country added to the general feel-good factor. It was voted European Car of the Year for 1988 by the biggest margin the contest had ever witnessed, and sold so well that 1 million had been built by 1990.

The 405 estate broadened the appeal of this great-to-drive Peugeot, retaining all the saloon's fine-handling prowess.

The 405's aerodynamics were another good reason that the car could muster great performance and economy in any form.

system it had limpet-like road adhesion. In contrast, the base 1.6 on its narrow tyres had an amazingly wind-cheating shape, with a drag co-efficient of just 0.29, so it was frugal *and* quite swift.

Peugeot had long been noted for its excellent estate cars, and the 405 didn't disappoint, with that option arriving in May 1988.

All in all, one of the all-round great affordable cars of the 1980s, and another winning design from a Peugeot that truly was a European leader.

Into the 1990s

The Peugeot 405 described on the previous two pages was not the last car to be launched in the 1980s, not by a long chalk. But it's probably the last significant new automotive product that would have become a familiar sight on our roads before the next decade dawned. Everything you'll read about in this section can, really, be considered as, most likely, cars we loved in the 1990s.

The ten years leading up to that momentous turn in millennia was destined to be the period when, slowly and cautiously, the rest of the '80s motor industry caught up with the pioneers of new car genres. We're talking specifically about the Multi-Passenger Vehicle (MPV) and the Sport-Utility Vehicle (SUV). The Renault Espace, Mitsubishi Space Wagon and, to a lesser degree, the Nissan Prairie had blazed the trail of versatile seating for five or seven people with a high roofline and a near-vertical tailgate. A full five years after this trio arrived, surprisingly there were still few other contenders, and

The seven-seater Toyota Previa would arrive in 1990, ready to capitalise on a new wave of enthusiasm for multi-passenger vehicles, or MPVs, a people-moving trend started by Renault, Nissan and Mitsubishi.

Land Rover's Discovery was a latecomer to the 4x4 market until then dominated by Japanese cars like the Mitsubishi Shogun and Isuzu Trooper, but its off-road prowess, and attractive design, quickly established it as the market leader.

the Prairie and Espace had both been revamped in 1988 and '89 respectively to smooth the abrupt corners of their uncompromisingly cubic profiles. Soon the Toyota Previa would join them and then, when the Ford Galaxy/VW Sharan pair arrived, the MPV floodgates would burst open.

As for SUVs, it was Japanese marques that had made the running, including those already featured in this book along with the Daihatsu Fourtrak, Nissan Patrol, Isuzu Trooper and Toyota Land Cruiser. By 1989, our own Land Rover finally had its riposte ready in the shape of the first Discovery, which shared its chassis with the venerable Range Rover, and just for a change the British 4x4 turned out to be one of the best of the bunch. With a family-friendly interior, awesome off-road prowess, and pretty accomplished road manners, it swiftly became the class bestseller and, indeed, for a long time the only European offering.

But the canny Japanese had already spotted the next niche: smaller 4x4 'leisure' vehicles. The first of these compact SUVs arrived in 1988 care of Daihatsu with its Sportrak, which offered urban (as opposed to rural) features like a five-speed gearbox and a 16-valve engine. It went some way to being like a normal car to drive on the road, but it was the 1989 Suzuki Vitara that changed the game, a totally usable four-wheel drive with a practical, high-roofed three-door hatchback body. It began paving the way for the many crossover vehicles we like so much today.

The tide of important new supermini launches in the first part of the 1980s ensured there was now a massive choice, and manufacturers took a breather later on as the many rivals squared up to one another. The most important of the second-generation wave arrived in 1989 when Ford totally overhauled its Fiesta, adding much more space in a body shape that was now offered with five as well as three doors, and a couple of economical new engines. With most of them now built at Dagenham, this would go on to monster sales in the years ahead.

By comparison, the upright little Mazda 121, which arrived on our shores in 1986, made no impact, although there was nothing much fundamentally wrong with it as a reliable city runabout. In 1991, though, this unassuming little grannymobile took on huge new significance after a licence-built South Korean edition returned to the UK as the very first Kia, the Pride.

A segment above it in the by-now well-defined motor industry hierarchy, Ford's Escort still ruled the family

This is the Suzuki Vitara, one of the first user-friendly 'lifestyle' sport-utility vehicles (SUVs) intended mainly for urban enjoyment with occasional forays on to rough tracks. Quite a practical little car, though.

A brand new Ford Fiesta arrived in 1989 ready for the '90s. There were new engines and a five-door option. This is the sporty, 110bhp XR2i model.

hatchback roost. In 1990, an all-new model failed to hit its target for style and performance, but even then the British trust in the Escort brand meant it enjoyed market-leading status. Meanwhile, this car and other popular alternatives like the Vauxhall Astra and VW Golf were under constant assault from similar cars.

In 1988 alone, the Fiat Tipo, Mazda 323F, Renault 19 and Volvo 440 were unveiled – all cars with a certain degree of individuality that intensified competition and boosted choice. In 1989, Rover had finally got its act together to take on the Escort head-on with the 200, a co-production with Honda. Great to drive and smart-looking, the 214 models were equipped with Rover's all-new 1.4-litre K Series aluminium twin-camshaft engine, while 216 versions featured a Honda 1.6 16-valve engine manufactured in Swindon.

Rover also manufactured Honda's edition of the car, called the Concerto, and it was clear that through their partnership, with an emphasis on quality and ease of ownership, Rover was on to a winner. The car was the basis for the 400 saloon, and soon there would be estate, coupé and convertible models in the 200/400 line-up.

Honda's Accord saloon was, at this stage, outside the scope of its Rover joint venture, and the fourth-generation version arrived in 1989 with 2.0- and 2.2-litre engines, excellent refinement, and the dubious novelty of a four-wheel steering system. As an import, relatively small numbers were sold here at relatively expensive prices. But that couldn't be said for the all-new Vauxhall Cavalier that debuted in 1988. It was a careful evolution of the earlier model, although the slow-selling estate model was dropped and a four-wheel drive system was

153

The Kia Pride, which made its UK debut in 1991, was a South Korean-made version of the Mazda 121. Little did we know that it would start the process that's turned Kia into a major worldwide success.

an interesting new option – one extremely effective in the 2.0-litre 16V performance model, which made great use of the additional grip to put its 150bhp to the road surface.

There was plenty of later-period activity in the executive and larger sports saloon sector. Alfa Romeo's 164 of 1988 was a departure for the Italian company, with front-wheel drive the mainstay layout and slick Pininfarina styling. Saab aficionados welcomed the 9000 CD in 1988, a

new saloon counterpart to run alongside the standard hatchback, with a gigantic rear luggage compartment. You would never have guessed these two cars used much of the same basic architecture.

In 1989, two large cars from France came on stream, the rather anodyne Peugeot 605 and the certainly very distinctive Citroën XM. Neither was destined to be a big seller in Britain, and the same was true for the Toyota Camry V6 of the same year, even though its engine and four-speed automatic gearbox were a peerlessly refined and silken combination; the car pointed to what could be expected in 1990 when Toyota launched its much-anticipated Lexus line.

Among more overtly sporting cars, there was much to admire in the Volkswagen Corrado, the Scirocco's successor, and also the Vauxhall Calibra with its highly aerodynamic shape. It was particularly comfortable for four passengers and, once endowed with a 201bhp turbocharged 2.0 engine, could be very fast. Both took their bow in 1989. That same year, Lotus's all-new Elan with front-wheel drive offered exceptional handling ('almost tediously good,' said one droll critic) but didn't sell too well, while the powerful, upmarket and beautifully

All the major European car manufacturers wanted a piece of the family hatchback action dominated by the Golf, Astra and Escort. This is the Tipo, Fiat's effort, launched in 1988; a good car then, no doubt, but not a great one.

Volvo's 440 had great appeal to the more mature and less excitable driver seeking something with more substance than most family cars. It could be had as both a hatchback and a saloon.

Rover finally got everything right with its 1989 200, co-developed with Honda, and it would give rise to a large range of related models that, for a short time at least, made the British marque a European front-runner.

built Mercedes-Benz SL became a smash hit around the world; it featured a world-first pop-up rollover-bar, G-force deployed if an accident was about to befall the two-seater roadster.

If you happened to be sitting in your old banger when one of these glamorous Mercs cruised past, you might have felt a bit miffed at the hand that motoring life had dealt you. But for anyone after a reasonably competent new car at rock bottom prices, the late 1980s had much in store. Okay, so the Yugo Sana of 1989 was pretty mediocre and, thanks to the Balkan War in the former Yugoslavia that saw its Serbian factory pounded with artillery (they made weaponry there as well as cars, apparently), it wasn't around for long. But the Škoda Favorit was a perky, front-drive newcomer from a Czechoslovakia soon to be freed from Soviet domination when the Berlin Wall collapsed and Communism imploded in 1990. And Proton was an all-new range of budget family cars from Malaysia; well ... apart from the fact that they were actually old Mitsubishis returned to the production lines for our grateful, cut-price consumption.

Alfa Romeo's executive flagship of the late 1980s and early 1990s was the 164: super car to drive, and great looking, but the ownership experience still lagged behind the trouble-free quality offered by BMW and Mercedes-Benz.

The purple golfing sweater in this picture maybe illustrates where Citroën saw its destiny with the new XM. Yet Britain's management classes weren't overly convinced by this radical looking French express of 1989, with its wacky suspension system and sensitive steering.

The Vauxhall Cavalier entered its third, and final, phase in 1988 with this new offering; four-wheel drive was a novelty that stirred interest but the main emphasis, as before, was on value, space and hassle-free running.

Lexus LS400, 1990: this large executive car, created from scratch by Toyota with no expense spared, would produce a Japanese contender to really give the German firms (and our own Jaguar) sleepless nights.

After the Capri had shrivelled away to nothing, and the elderly Opel Manta had staggered on to 1989, Vauxhall reinvigorated the market for sleek four-seater coupés that year with this, the Calibra.

Volkswagen's 1989 Corrado was another newcomer to the ranks of very late 1980s coupés, a car loved for its shape, performance, comfort and reassuring Volkswagen build quality.

Just a few months before the Berlin Wall was breached and Communism imploded, Czechoslovakia's Škoda showed it could make a thoroughly modern car, with the front-wheel drive Favorit hatchback.